CH00661775

Philosophers' Dogs

Philosophers' Dogs

Samuel Dodson and Rosie Benson

unbound

First published in 2021

Unbound
Level 1, Devonshire House, One Mayfair Place, London W1J 8AJ
www.unbound.com

Text design by PDQ Digital Media Solutions Ltd.

A CIP record for this book is available from the British Library

ISBN 978-1-80018-066-6 (hardback)
ISBN 978-1-80018-067-3 (ebook)

Printed in Great Britain by CPI Group (UK)

1 3 5 7 9 8 6 4 2

For all dogs. You are very, very good. Oh yes you are, oh yes you are.

Contents

Introduction

Are tennis balls always real? Is it possible to be a good dog? Do we act freely, catching Frisbees and sticks of our own volition? Or are our actions, our decisions – to eat rotten apples, to bark at the cat – predetermined? Is a bark truly worse than a bite? Where does our urge to chase the postman come from? What is it to *know* that you have behaved well rather than merely to believe it?

These are questions that have been pondered for many thousands of years by some of the brightest minds ever to walk on four legs. The answers have led to countless breakthroughs in what humans might describe as 'philosophy'. But, before we go on, let us pause to consider what we mean by this term.

Humans are told that the literal meaning of 'philosophy' is 'the love of wisdom'. But this is a simple case of canine–*Homo sapiens* misinterpretation. The classic, ancient canine meaning of the word stems from the base etymological construction *phur* – meaning, well, fur. To truly understand philosophy, you must remember its core meaning, the root injunction, which is 'to think with fur'.

Already, fur-lacking humans may feel at a disadvantage. But fear not! As Professor Friend, one of our foremost canine philosophers and key consultant for this book, notes, 'Just because one does not have fur, it does not mean one cannot think with fur. All that is required is that you put aside petty human concerns and worries – thoughts of mortgages, cutlery and needlessly frightening vacuum cleaners – and concentrate instead on life's big questions like, which of us can truly be described as a "good" dog?'

For Professor Friend – and, indeed, all fur-thinkers (or 'philoso-furs') who have gone before her – philosophical thinking begins with a moment of wonder. This wondering can often be achieved through wandering – also known as 'walkies' – as we try to make sense of the world around us.

For many, a desire to investigate the world is the first paw-step into the world of philosophy. This investigation can take place with the help of a probing snoot ('nose') and a good sense of smell; but it can also be done by asking questions.

The major figures in ancient philosophy, including Socrates' dog, Socra-fleas, and Aristotle's pooch, Arisdoggle, stressed the importance of questioning the world. Why, for example, should we give our paw to someone simply because they command it? What happens to us after we cross the rainbow bridge and go to live on the farm? Is it possible to judge free will in a world where treats seem accessible only by obeying orders?

Some philosophical puppers, like Bernard the Saint and Sun Shih-Tzu, went further, believing that we should catalogue the thoughts and questions of *all* dogs, and encourage *all* of canine-kind to ask questions of the world. By inspiring others, they saw the potential for eventual canine liberation from the oppression of humans.

Sadly, the leash of mankind is hard to shake off.

What's more, the human ego is a fragile thing, as Freud's dog, Sigmutt, would one day teach us. No human could ever stand the idea that the true meaning of existence might be discovered by a being so much smaller and furrier, and which often delights in eating its own excrement.

And so, from the very start, and to preserve the social order in a way that benefited humans, the first philosophical thoughts of dogs have been co-opted and stolen by their masters, who, with simple modifications, attempted to pass them off as their own.

Let us be clear: all human 'philosophers' stole their best ideas from their dogs.

It's true.* From Aristotle and Confucius, Marcus Aurelius and John Locke, to Mary Wollstonecraft and Karl Marx, each and every human philosopher since time immemorial has lifted their best ideas and insights from their four-legged friends. Not only that, but they've shamelessly chopped and changed their dogs' original philosophical thoughts to make them sound more human – for that, read 'more foolish'.

That this reality is not taught to every philosophy student, dog 'owner' or dog lover – indeed to every person living on this earth today – is a travesty.

Fortunately, many canine scholars, led by Professor Friend, have been digging up more than bones in recent years to try and piece together the true history of the 'love of wisdom'. Their labours have not been in vain, and the works of some of history's greatest canines have finally come to light. It is therefore our dog's honour to present to you, dear readers, a true history of canine philosophy, fully illustrated with paw-traits of some of the very good dogs who played such an important role in making it.

An important note to human readers
Your introduction to the philosophers' dogs to whom we owe so much lies in the following pages. It is important that you complete your studies in this long-neglected field, but if, at any time, you hear the sound of a dog in distress, we encourage you to tend to said dog at once, providing them with whatever bones, kibbles, squeaky toys or belly rubs they may require. It's the least you can do, after all.

* Not necessarily true.

2

Socrates

'The only thing I can know is that I know nothing about who pooed on the rug.'

Name: Socrates
Dog's name: Socra-fleas
Breed: Greek harehound
Born: 470 BCE
Went to live on the farm: 399 BCE
Age in dog years: 297

Principles
- Knowledge of where treats are hidden is a virtue.
- No dog is a bad dog knowingly or willingly.

Likes/favourite pastimes
- Chasing the discus
- Eating laurel wreaths
- Sticking head out the side of the chariot

Special interest: notorious for asking for the ball to be thrown, but never returning the ball

Impact on philosophy

So-called philosophers have been stealing the best ideas from their dogs since ancient times – and probably before that. Perhaps the best-known stealer of canine ideas was a man named Socrates, born in Athens around 470 BCE. Humans (wrongly) consider Socrates to be the grandfather – or perhaps even founding father – of philosophy.

Yet it is Socrates' harehound, Socra-fleas, to whom the real philosophical debt is owed. As a young pup, he had been a brave fighter in the Pelo-paw-nnesian wars against the cat-worshipping Spartans. But his experiences of conflict made him reflective. He began to ask questions such as, 'Why are we fighting in a war, when we could be going for a walk?'

Soon, barking questions was all Socra-fleas was doing. Yet unlike the thinkers, canine and human alike, who came before him, Socra-fleas wasn't interested in merely asking questions about the material world – 'Is that a piece of food, and can I eat it?' Rather, he wanted to know how dogs could live good, 'moral' lives.

For Socra-fleas, to live a good life and be considered a good dog, you have to know what virtue is. And for Socra-fleas, virtue was knowledge. He didn't think that dogs did bad things because they were bad; he thought they did them because they didn't know better – probably because they hadn't been taught or trained well enough by their idle 'owners'. He thought that if a dog truly knew the right or good thing to do in any situation, then they would always take that option. For example, if a dog is never told that it should not steal the sirloin steak from a human's plate, the dog cannot be said to be a bad dog if it does, for it was ignorant of the correct course of action.

But how can we know what the correct course of action is in any given situation? You might think that the dog in the above scenario had done wrong – by taking the sirloin steak without asking. But why would you think that? What if the human about to eat the steak was obese, or had many more sirloin steaks in the larder, so likely to become so? What if the human's doctor (a sort of vet for humans) had told that person they should avoid eating red meat for their health? In this light, so far from being a bad act, taking the steak might be said to be a *moral* act, if doing so helped the human live more healthily.

It may not be clear to us, in any given instance, what the right or wrong course of action is. Yet we are only ever given answers if we ask questions. This is what Socra-fleas was trying to show us.

So, for Socra-fleas, a good life was one spent in pursuit of the truth. This is what he meant when he said, 'The unexamined life is not worth living, and never forget to examine a tree you pass either – only then may you uncover the squirrels hiding in its branches.'

Unfortunately, Socra-fleas' habit of barking questions – often quite loudly – started to annoy some important Athenians. It wasn't just the noise that annoyed them, you understand; it was that human beings don't enjoy being made to feel less intelligent than a dog. So the decision was taken to bring some trumped-up charges against Socra-fleas, so that his accusers could do away with this interrogative harehound and begin the long process of passing off his ideas as his master's.

In one of the first recorded cases of human–canine copyright infringement, Socrates' dog was put on trial, purportedly for pooing on the rug, in 399 BCE. The case was brought by three of the cruellest dog wardens of Athens – Lycon, Antyus, and Meletus – who accused Socrates' dog of pooing not just on their rugs, but on their lawns as well. During his trial Socra-fleas established one of the most important tenets of philosophy: namely, that all philosophical thought begins with an admission of ignorance.

'The only thing I can know is that I know nothing about who pooed on the rug,' Socra-fleas barked, before going further and arguing that the wardens should reward him by giving him free meals for life.

As you can imagine, the wardens – and the fearsome bureau-cats who controlled them – took none too kindly to Socra-fleas or his master. Both were sent to live on the farm across the rainbow bridge.

Though first recorded by Plato's Molosser (Fido-rus – see page 9), the original scrolls containing the accounts of Socra-fleas' trial were stolen and bastardised by Plato. In a classic human move, Plato attributed this founding philosophical principle of ignorance to his mate Socrates, to whom he owed a number of pints (and a rooster – but that's another story). It was in this rewritten, false version of events that mankind first encountered the idea that the only thing a man or dog can know is that he knows nothing.

While it may be true that humans really do know very little about the world, for dogs it is only true that they will try to *feign* ignorance – pretending to know less than they do in order to serve some higher purpose. This is known as Socratic irony, and it is impossible fully to appreciate human–canine relations without some consideration of it in action.

For example, when a human discovers a pungent pile of vomit in the basket of their faithful hound, their instinct so often is to point at the dog. Yet a dog, practising Socratic irony, will cock its head on one side, questioningly, in an attempt to force the human to ask questions of its own role in the vomit's existence. Would there be any vomit at all, the dog will encourage the human to consider, if they had been let out into the garden when they were waiting by the door? And, in so many ways, is it not the *human*'s fault that the big box of After Eight mints was left within easy reach upon the low-rise coffee table? After a silent exchange of glances between dog and human, it is the human who must take responsibility for the entire ordeal and begin cleaning up. It is, ultimately, their problem after all.

Many humans have tried to perfect this technique themselves. Yet in numerous cases it has been corrupted, with people frequently forgetting they do not need to *be* ignorant for this subtle and revealing technique to work.

Related topics: irony, ancient Greece, pooper scoopers

Plato

'Fur-losophy begins in wonder – for example, the wonder you find in butterflies.'

Name: Plato
Dog's name: Fido-rus
Breed: Molosser
Born: 428 BCE
Went to live on the farm: 348 BCE
Age in dog years: 337

Principles
- A true republic should be run by dogs and full of licks.
- Of all the gods, Dog is the best friend of humankind, the helper and healer of all ills that stand in the way of human happiness.
- We should think more carefully rather than be led by our instincts.

Likes/favourite pastimes
- Looking at beautiful things that possess the 'form of the good', like tennis balls
- Practising self-control, reasonableness and independent thinking
- Examining all aspects of life, especially aromatic cowpats

Special interest: chasing butterflies

Impact on philosophy
If we could conceive of the perfect form of government for society, what would it look like? For one of the great canine philosophers, the answer was obvious: there should be more dogs in it.

Plato's dog, Fido-rus, was one of Socrates' dog's greatest students. But he was a fantastic philosopher (and a very, very good dog) in his own right too. He was fascinated by questions that asked how we should govern ourselves, and tried to describe the perfect society. He believed the ideal state should be made up of a thinking elite (philosophers' dogs), who would be protected by the strongest guard dogs for defence against possible attacks by cats or squirrel invasions. Beneath the thinkers and the guard dogs, you would have the working dogs, whose job it would be to make sure sheep were in the right place, and all bones buried in well-dug holes. Finally, beneath the working dogs, you could have humans, who might be allowed to perform important duties, like petting the dogs and giving them belly rubs.

For Fido-rus, this hierarchy was based on a dog's wisdom – something he felt was incredibly important. He once observed, 'Wise dogs bark because they have something to say; foolish dogs woof because they have to woof at something.'

In his ideal society, the wisest, 'thinking' dogs would be allowed to immerse themselves in philosophy to consider the answers to important questions such as, 'Is it better to play fetch with a tennis ball or a discus?' They could then make rational decisions (about whether we play with the ball or discus on any given day), and so govern the world effectively.

Plato's dog believed that successful states would have a canine 'fur-losopher king' as head of state. This was because he saw that dogs look naturally towards the light, are all very good boys and girls, and are uninterested in foolish human things like money. As a result they would be incorruptible.

He described this type of state in one of his most important works, *The Republick* (heavy emphasis on *lick*). In his ideal society, dogs would be free to lick any and all faces, regardless of whether they had recently eaten a cowpat or some suspicious and long-discarded piece of meat.

Unfortunately, no canine has ever been able to live under such a government. Instead, Plato, that classic canine-idea stealer, flipped his dog's ideas to such an extent that he wound up arguing for men – not dogs – at the top of any system of government – and look how well *that's* worked out over the past 2,500 years.

Despite this, Plato's dog continued to ponder important questions. In fact, he quickly became a great theorist on relationships. His collection of barkings, *The Symposium*, is an attempt to explain what love really is, and why dogs love their 'owners' – even when humans steal their best ideas and do not share their yummy-looking moussaka. *The Symposium* tells the story of a dinner party given by Wag-athon, a handsome dog who invites a group of his friends around to eat kibble, drink from muddy puddles and bark about love.

The guests all have different views about what love is. One of the most interesting theories Fido-rus presents goes like this. When you fall in love with a human, what's really going on is that you've seen in that person a quality you haven't got – usually, that they have opposable thumbs and are tall enough to open packets of biscuits hidden away in hard-to-reach cupboards. But the reverse is also true: humans love dogs because they see in them qualities that *they* do not possess. Dogs can find joy and excitement in the smallest things, like butterflies or oddly shaped sticks, whereas humans need constant stimulation and are prone to boredom. What's more, a dog will always show love, even when a human expresses anger or hate.

In this way, a dog can help a human to grow to their full potential; and in return a human can help a dog to eat more biscuits. Fido-rus barked, 'Of all the gods, Dog is the best friend of humankind, the helper and healer of all ills that stand in the way of human happiness.'

These types of ideas were typical of Fido-rus, who fully embraced the mantra of his tutor, Socra-fleas, to question the world around us. Fido-rus loved using his nose to thoroughly examine all aspects of the world around him – from love and society through to nature itself, and the various forms it can take (particularly cowpats). He famously barked, 'Fur-losophy begins in wonder – for example, the wonder you find in butterflies.'

Despite trying to paw many of his dog's ideas off as his own, Plato at least recognised the groundbreaking importance of his canine companion's barkings. He even named one of his books *Fidorus* after his faithful hound. It is once again thanks to centuries of human misspelling that people mistakenly believe this book is called *Phaedrus*. Now, at last, you know the truth.

Related topics: government, love, butterflies

Aristotle

'Human happiness depends upon dogs.'

Name: Aristotle
Dog's name: Arisdoggle
Breed: Border collie
Born: 384 BCE
Went to live on the farm: 322 BCE
Age in dog years: 261

Principles
- Philosophising is best undertaken while on walkies.
- A virtuous life is one that strikes a perfect balance – the so-called 'golden (retriever) mean'.

Likes/favourite pastimes
- Using all senses to investigate and understand everything in the world, especially sausages
- Watching dramatic plays at the amphitheatre (and barking at any dogs that come on stage)

Special interest: supporting the happiness of humans through plentiful, enthusiastic face licks

Impact on philosophy

As far as the so-called 'grandfathers' of philosophy go, few have been so rudely overlooked as Aristotle's dog. A student of Plato's dog Fido-rus, and so therefore indirectly a student of Socrates' dog Socra-fleas, few philosophical dogs have been as influential as Arisdoggle. Socrates' dog had been a great barker, and Plato's dog an excellent tail-wagger, but Arisdoggle was interested in everything. This could be seen generally, in the way he stopped to sniff every plant, rock or post that he encountered on any walk, sometimes even returning to sniff the same item multiple times after walking on for a few steps.

Like all great students (or dogs, for that matter), Arisdoggle took on aspects of his master's teachings and philosophy while also striking out independently and becoming very much his own dog, conducting philosophy in his own way. While Plato's dog was ultimately content to philosophise from a soft bed, or a comfy and obliging lap, Arisdoggle wanted to explore the reality we experience through the senses. So, to understand what a sausage is, you need to look at real sausages, and sniff them, and then taste them. And then repeat the process as many times as you can get away with. There is no point, he reasoned, in just thinking abstractly about the 'form' of sausages. Rather, for Arisdoggle, what is important is the world we sense around us, and the relationships, friendships and (yes) sausages that exist within it.

'Dogs began to do philosophy,' he woofed, 'even as they do now, because of wonder. At first because they wondered about the strange things right in front of them, like suspicious-looking buckets, asking "What on earth is that?" and "Why and how does it exist?" Philosophy begins by asking these questions, and using all the senses at your disposal to investigate their possible answers.'

It was perhaps this fervent desire to explore every aspect of the world that led Arisdoggle to develop what is known as the peripatetic school of philosophy, from the ancient Greek περιπατητικός (*peripatētikós*), which means 'of walking' or 'given to going on walkies'.

'Explore the world under the power of your own paws,' Arisdoggle instructs us. 'There is something marvellous in all things of nature, like sticks. There's enough to give any dog a major excite.'

It's perhaps unsurprising that Arisdoggle had a committed group of followers and students, including Alexander the Great Dane. But what's interesting about this particular philosophical pooch is that he didn't just try to influence his canine compatriots; he also did his best to improve the lives and well-being of the humans around him.

Indeed, Arisdoggle realised early on that human happiness was often hindered by a lack of soft fur to stroke, and just as often improved by lots of sloppy, enthusiastic licks.

It was during one particularly enthusiastic face-licking session, while out with his master for one of their extended philosophical walkies, that Arisdoggle barked a particularly important observation: 'Human happiness depends upon dogs.'

You can see Arisdoggle's teachings being followed by all dogs to this very day. And while humans may be content to sit on sofas, watching endless television series and staring at screens, dogs continue to try, as they have been trying for millennia, to help them understand the importance of going on walkies. Whether this is done by picking up leads in their mouths or scratching at the new paint on the front door, it is the sign of a virtuous dog, following Arisdoggle-an ethics, trying simply to enhance their 'owner's' happiness.

But what exactly do we mean by happiness, or virtue?

Face licks are obviously a part of it, but Arisdoggle's term for happiness was *eudaemonia*, which essentially means to be living and doing well. This is something that goes beyond fleeting pleasures like face-licking or rolling in particularly pungent poo. It also goes beyond desire for food or the company of good humans who may provide food, for praise and the esteem of the pack – human or canine – for good health or access to tennis balls. For Arisdoggle, merely having all these things is not enough to achieve *eudaemonia*; instead, one must have *earned* them. He barked, 'Dignity does not come from possessing treats, but from deserving them.'

He also stressed that while possessing food, or receiving belly rubs and so on, could provide a dog with momentary pleasure, it would never be enough to lead to everlasting happiness. And it was for this reason that he once observed, 'One treat does not make a dinner.'

To become truly good, to achieve true happiness, dogs must think not only of full food bowls or aromatic cowpats, but of their society – or pack – as a whole. How can one contribute to society in a way that is paw-sitive and thoughtful? For Arisdoggle, this was about being *virtuous*, using the rational mind to control and direct our activities. In particular, this idea encourages dogs not to act on their most basic urges: 'It is the mark of an educated dog to be able to catch a Frisbee without eating it.'

To illustrate virtue, let us take an example of a common occurrence in canine life. Think of the virtue of bravery that is called for when a suspicious pair of Cub Scouts approaches the house to hawk their overpriced cookies. Any good dog will know that it must be prepared to put its own life at risk in order to save the family (pack) from a dastardly attack. A foolhardy dog has no concern whatsoever for its own safety. It might rush unnecessarily into a dangerous situation, perhaps through the cat flap. It might then get stuck in the cat flap and the fire brigade might have to be called. This – it should be plain – is not true bravery, according to Arisdoggle. Rather, it is reckless risk-taking. At the other end of the spectrum, of course, you have the cowardly dog, who will hide with his tail between his legs under the kitchen table until the Cub Scouts have left the premises. Perhaps he will even leave a little treat for the family to clean up. That is, if the

family haven't been brutally murdered by the Cub Scouts. Now, in the same situation, a truly brave or courageous dog will still feel fear – it may want to cower in terror inside a box somewhere – but crucially, it will also be able to overcome this fear and take action – standing *behind* the front door, perhaps, and barking incessantly until the Cub Scouts are driven off, never to return. Here, bravery is halfway between foolhardiness and cowardice, and, according to Arisdoggle, this is the golden (retriever) mean.

Striking this perfect balance in any situation should always be seen as a dog's ultimate goal in life. We become virtuous, Arisdoggle says, by practising virtue. If we teach young puppies good habits and tricks, those habits and tricks will become second nature. Yet this should not be seen as a one-off stage of education; it is vital that we continue our training and education, learning and repeating our virtuous tricks. And so, turning his attention to old dogs and new tricks, and emphasising the lifelong commitment to virtue we should all make, he woofed, 'We are what tricks we repeatedly do. Excellent training, therefore, is not a single trick, but a habit.'

Related topics: virtue, happiness, Cub Scouts

Confucius

'It does not matter how long you must wait to eat the roast duck, as long as you do not stop trying to eat the roast duck.'

Name: Confucius
Dog's name: Con-fur-cius
Breed: Tibetan terrier
Born: 551 BCE
Went to live on the farm: 479 BCE
Age in dog years: 301

Principles
- It is more shameful to distrust a dog than to be deceived by one, even if it means your roast duck somehow disappears.
- Do not do to dogs what you would not have them do to you. For this reason, humans should never chase a dog with a broom.
- Loyalty, caring for other dogs and showing respect for family and friends are some of the most important values a dog can have.

Likes/favourite pastimes
- Practising the ancient canine martial art of kung-fur
- Paw-print calligraphy
- Teaching ordinary dogs extraordinary tricks

Special interest: digging holes instead of seeking revenge

Impact on philosophy

It's not just dogs in the Western world who have had a profound influence on philosophy. While philosophers in ancient Greece were stealing ideas from their four-legged companions, philosophical thoughts were also being woofed – and ripped off – in Asia.

Of all the Eastern philosophical puppers, few have had such an extraordinary influence on the world as Con-fur-cius.

Con-fur-cius was an ordinary mutt who dedicated himself to training. As a puppy he sought to learn and master the Six Arts: howling, ritualised tummy tickles, chasing chariots, fetching arrows, counting ticks (also known as arith-mutt-ticks) and creating beautiful paw-print calligraphy (callig-woof-y) by artfully decorating his 'owner's' recently cleaned hall with mud harvested from his recent walkies.

This dedication led Con-fur-cius to believe that, through training, all dogs – even ordinary ones – were capable of performing great tricks. If all dogs went to puppy school, he thought, they would not only acquire wisdom, but be able to transform canine society.

For many years, Con-fur-cius, serving in the court of the local duke in what is now the Shandong province of China, tried to convince ruling dogs and humans of his beliefs. But the duke seemed more interested in making sure his cats enjoyed chasing little balls with tiny bells in them than in helping either his canine or human subjects to become better educated. Con-fur-cius was alienated by the excesses of the duke, and when the duke forgot to offer him a portion of sacrificial meat (which Con-fur-cius had reason to believe would be *very* tasty), he left the court and went on a series of long walkies across China, lasting twelve years.

It was in this time of self-imposed exile that Con-fur-cius began to amass a whole pack of students and disciples. On his walkies he stressed to his students the importance of filial piety – respecting older dogs and reverencing the family, by which he meant guarding the family home from interloping postmen, waiting calmly to be fed and sometimes even allowing the humans to sit on the chairs and sofa.

Like many philosophers' dogs from the ancient world, Con-fur-cius didn't write much of his work down. In part, this is what made it so easy for humans to pass off his best ideas as their own. What we know of his teachings, therefore, comes mostly from what was written down by his students. The most important catalogue of his teachings is in a book originally called the *Anelects* (though it is worth noting that this is the name given by rather prudish humans, who altered the original title, *Anal-licks*, in order to lessen the number of references to the essential business of licking one's genitals).

This important book carries many woofs of wisdom from Con-fur-cius, many of which will be familiar to dogs to this day. Here is a short list.

- A dog is a true friend who never betrays.
- The more a dog eats good food, the better will be his world and the world at large.
- By nature, dogs are nearly all alike; by practice, they grow to be wide apart.
- Real knowledge is to know the extent of a human's ignorance.

Some of Con-fur-cius's barkings may be recognisable to some humans. For instance, he cautioned against taking vengeance on others – even if, by others, one meant the yappy Chihuahua who once ran off with your Frisbee. He barked, 'Before you embark on a journey of revenge, dig two holes. And then dig some more holes. Soon you will have forgotten why you were thinking of going on any journey at all, and you will have lots of holes to bury bones in. You may also find bones previously buried. Who needs revenge when you have bones and holes to dig?'

Con-fur-cius was not concerned with trivial human distractions like making money. For him, actions were far more important, and he believed that if he simply behaved well, walking to heel and sniffing the bottoms of others as they might sniff his, he would inspire others.

Many short barkings and woofs of wisdom have been attributed to Con-fur-cius over the years, but none is more important than his 'golden rule': 'Do not do to others what you do not want done to yourself.'

At its heart, this moral principle may seem like a no-brainer: be kind, loving and forgiving to others, because that's how you would like people to behave towards you. And it's a rule that nearly all dogs put into practice every day, often without getting treats in return. It's the basic reason a dog will return your stick whenever you throw it. After all, they know how much you must love your stick (they would love that stick very much if it was theirs), and so they know that, were they foolish enough to throw it a long way away, they would definitely want someone to fetch it for them.

Ultimately, the golden rule encourages a dog to take personal responsibility for its actions with regard to the people around it. If you have ever come home from work, exhausted and despondent, and found that your dog comes and places its head in your lap, licks your hand and looks up at you with kind, doleful eyes, you can be pretty sure your pooch knows its Con-fur-cius. A more extreme example is if you've ever accidentally kicked or tripped over your dog only to find it pressing up against you, anxious to protect you from invisible kicking monsters. Some 2,000 years after Con-fur-cius went to live on the farm across the rainbow bridge, these instances of devotion are moments in which dogs continue faithfully to embody Con-fur-cius's golden rule – of which English poet Alexander Poop once barked, 'To err is human; to forgive, canine.'

Related topics: callig-woof-y, the golden rule, bones

Sun Tzu

'The supreme art of walks is to remove the leash without asking.'

Name: Sun Tzu
Dog's name: Sun Shih-Tzu
Breed: shih-tzu
Born: 544 BCE
Went to live on the farm: 496 BCE
Age in dog years: 197

Principles
- The art of walks is a matter of life and death.
- True canine leaders stand for the virtues of cuddles, tummy tickles, serenity, courage and being a good dog.
- All walkies are based on deception.

Likes/favourite pastimes
- Running the lead round and round humans until they are completely bound and trapped
- Begging to go outside to wee, without actually needing to wee at all, and so being able to sniff different blades of grass intently for hours on end while a human waits in the rain
- Plotting effective strategies to acquire more food

Special interest: barking loudly at his enemies (postmen and cats) to make them believe he is nearby and terribly frightening

Impact on philosophy
Sun Shih-Tzu was an ancient Chinese philosophical dog credited with developing perhaps the most influential barking thesis of walking strategy: *The Art of Walkies*. Though bastardised by his 'owner' into a book about military tactics, the original work, as developed by Sun Shih-Tzu, has affected all of Western and east-Asian philosophy.

The dogs of Chinese military generals in the sixth and fifth centuries BCE tended to focus on aggression – on biting, snarling and barking loudly – but Sun Shih-Tzu's revelatory work focuses on alternatives to anger; specifically, on tactics and strategies that will in the long run be more effective at getting dogs what they want (food and walkies) while avoiding things they don't want (being put in cages or told they are bad dogs).

For example, after an encounter with one particularly aggressive toddler, Sun Shih-Tzu discovered that by temporarily submitting, rolling over and allowing his tummy to be tickled and stroked (albeit too strongly), he could avoid a confrontation with other foes, including the allies of said toddler and its dreadful parents. Rather than snarl at the toddler and risk being struck on the nose, Sun Shih-Tzu endured unwanted and inexpert tummy rubs which enabled enabled him to plot his escape at the earliest opportunity.

Sun Shih-Tzu's strategies are still used by dogs around the world today. A classic example is the use of deceit to gain access to forbidden territory, such as the garden or that comfortable king-size bed. Sun Shih-Tzu taught that, by standing beside the French doors and acting as if you need the toilet, humans will be deceived into thinking you need to go outside – at which point, you are able to explore and roam the garden for as long as you please, sniffing at whichever blades of grass you like and discovering rotten apples to eat, with no repercussions. The only non-waiting option available to the human (or 'foe', in this instance) is that of coming into the garden to chase you – at which point victory is assured. You will have forced the human out of its secure location into an engagement with you on your own terms, in the landscape of your choosing.

Here it is worth considering one of the core tenets of Sun Shih-Tzu's philosophy: 'The whole secret lies in confusing the human, so that he cannot fathom our real intent – to avoid capture and remain outside.' While some humans have mistakenly taken these antics for playful disobedience, it is vital to remember that dogs are in fact observing a strict discipline – engaging only on their own terms and controlling the situation for their own ends. Similarly, by feigning weakness or illness when you are in fact strong, Sun Shih-Tzu taught that it was possible to deceive humans into giving you their sympathy and more treats, and also making them far less likely to remove you from the king-size bed or sofa.

Sun Shi-Tzu also stressed the importance of intelligence operatives and espionage to the universal walkies effort. In practical terms, this entails staring at the cupboard where the dog food is kept, as well as sitting very close to humans while they eat their own food. It also means listening carefully to what humans say, and responding as needed whenever the letters w-a-l-k are used in any combination at all.

While much of his work focuses on preparations for walkies and gaining greater access to food, *The Art of Walkies* also discusses tactics that may be deployed by canines while perambulating with their so-called masters.

For instance, Sun Shih-Tzu taught the importance of agility as well as discipline. While one is on the leash, it is appropriate to walk obediently to heel. However, once the leash is removed, one may bound away as quickly as possible – to eat leftover curry, perhaps, or to meet and sniff the bottoms of strange dogs a little way ahead, or else to chase squirrels in a neighbouring woodland. Hence, the famous injunction: 'Let your plans be dark and impenetrable as night, and when you move, run away like a thunderbolt.'

Sun Shih-Tzu's teachings were praised and employed by east-Asian canines from the very start, and with the help of various salty old merchant seadogs word soon spread across the world. For centuries, his tactics have been used by sheepdogs in their daily battles with the great woolly peril. Though always outnumbered, sheepdogs are able to defend existing positions, divide their enemies and move them around difficult terrain, all while maintaining the agility and speed necessary to evade any counter-attacks. Importantly, sheepdogs remember this crucial teaching from Sun Shih-Tzu: 'The expert in herding moves the sheep, and is not moved by them.'

Though misattributed to a human mind – and mistitled as a result – *The Art of Walkies* continues to influence many competitive endeavours in the world of culture, politics, business and sports. It is said that Barack Obama's dogs kept a copy of the work in their kennel, and their close reading of it proved a vital ingredient in Obama's sweeping and historic victory in the 2008 US presidential campaign.

Related topics: walkies, strategy, agility

Marcus Aurelius

> *'Very little is needed to make you wag your tail; it is all within yourself in your way of thinking.'*

Name: Marcus Aurelius
Dog's name: Barkus Aurelius
Breed: Spinone Italiano
Born: 121 CE
Went to live on the farm: 180 CE
Age in dog years: 245

Principles
- Dog Stoicism, which means learning to accept and come to terms with the existence of cats.
- Happiness can be found at all times and in all places, but belly rubs help.

Likes/favourite pastimes
- Chewing the emperor's new clothes
- Becoming one with nature by chasing squirrels
- Wagging one's tail as the universe intended

Special interest: meditating while licking one's genitals

Impact on philosophy

The Stoics were a group of philosophical dogs generally found cocking their legs around the Stoa in ancient Athens. A key part of their vision was that each dog should aspire to be nature's best friend, as well as man's. Dogs should fully understand the interconnectedness of the physical world, seeing the necessity in all things (even cats), and be able to answer any conceivable question such as, 'How many pieces of kibble make a pile big enough to fill a bowl?' (The answer, of course, is that there is never enough kibble, and the bowl must always be refilled).

The chief philosophical pupper of Stoicism was Barkus Aurelius – dog to the Roman emperor, commander of the bone stores of the north, best friend to his human 'owner', father to a neutered son, husband to a spayed wife and inspiration to Russell Crowe in *Gladiator*.

A central theme of Barkus' *Meditations (While Licking Your Genitals)* is the importance of finding inner peace and understanding your place in the wider context of the universe. It was crucial, he believed, to maintain focus and be without distractions, to be able to ignore discarded cartons of takeaway food and concentrate on strong ethical principles such as 'being a good dog'. Indeed, in one of his earliest meditations, produced on a bone-burying campaign during the Feline–Roman wars, he barked, 'Don't waste the rest of your time here worrying about other dogs, unless it affects the common good. It will keep you from doing anything useful. You'll be too preoccupied with whose bottom so-and-so is sniffing, and why, and what they're thinking, or what toys they have, or what they're eating, and all the other things that throw you off and keep you from focusing on your own bone.'

Barkus advocated finding one's place in the universe. He saw that everything came from nature, and would return to it in due course. Imploring all dogs to focus on the things under their control, he once woofed, 'The happiness of your life depends upon the quality of your walkies'– surely an adage we can all live by.

Interestingly, his Stoic ideas often involve avoiding indulgence in sensory experiences, in the belief that this will free a dog from the pains and pleasures of the material world. Thus, he believed dogs should not covet fancy jackets or collars, or trouble themselves with badgers or smelly cats. He claimed that the only way a dog can be harmed by others is if it allows itself to be overpowered by its own reactions – noting, 'One should always ignore the Chihuahua that barks and bares its teeth as you pass it in the park, and focus only on the walkies you are currently taking.'

The questions that the *Meditations* attempt to answer are primarily metaphysical and ethical. Why are we here? How should we wag our tails? How can we ensure that we are good dogs? How can we protect ourselves against the stresses and pressures of daily life? How should we deal with the pain caused by the existence of cats? How can we live with the knowledge that, soon, the food in our bowls will no longer exist? Is it possible to accept that, much later, we will all take a one-way trip to the vets?

To answer these questions, Barkus advocates following what he called the 'discipline of perception'. This requires maintaining absolute objectivity of thought, so that we see things dispassionately for what they are. A cat is just a cat, not necessarily an enemy. An empty food bowl is, likewise, just an empty bowl – it does not have to be the source, or cause, of anxiety.

Barkus acknowledges that this is difficult, especially when you consider that cats are *almost certainly* plotting against us. All the time. But he explains the problem using a metaphor that is still used by stoical dogs alive today: objects and events in the world around us bombard us with impressions. As they do so, they produce a mental impression. From this the mind generates a perception, which might best be compared to a muddy paw-print left on a newly fitted white carpet. Ideally, this print will be an accurate and faithful representation of the original paw. But it may not; it may be blurred, or somewhat faint, after the application of surprisingly ineffective high-end cleaning compounds.

Misleading perceptions can lead to inappropriate value judgments: the designation of something as 'good' or 'evil' when it is neither. For example, your impression that the postman is about to deliver something is just that – an impression or report conveyed to you by your senses about an event in the outside world – in this case the street outside your house. By contrast, your perception that the postman is absolutely evil and a threat to everyone in the household includes not only an impression, but also an interpretation imposed upon that initial impression by the powers of your mind. It is by no means the only possible interpretation, and – like the muddy paw-print – it may not accurately or fairly represent reality. You are also not obliged to accept it. In fact, you may be a good deal better off if you decline to do so. In other words, it is not postmen or deliveries – or even cats – that are the issue, but rather the interpretations we place on them. Our duty is therefore to exercise stricter control over the faculty of perception, with the aim of protecting our minds from error.

Barkus also stressed the difference between those things that are within our control (like our ability to accept or ignore our perception of outside events) and those things that are outside of control – the things that are done to us. Dogs control their own actions and are responsible for them, whether that be barking at the postman or rolling in an aromatic cowpat. If we act wrongly – bite others or not walk to heel – then we have done serious harm to ourselves, as these are not the actions of a 'good' dog.

By contrast, things outside our control have no ability to harm us – even if the spoilt child pulls our tail too firmly, or the human leaves the house and you have no idea whether it has been gone for five minutes or five years.

These things are not within our control because Barkus believed in the existence of Logos, a fate or destiny. The universe is following a set path that we may not alter. 'You may think of this,' Barkus barked,

as a long walk on which you are kept on a lead. The human is following a path that is sometimes muddy, and sometimes contains frightening things like upturned buckets or gaps in the hedge. Yet, because you are on the lead, and because the human is walking at a brisk pace, there is no way for you to change the course you are on. Of course, this is not to say one lacks free will. All dogs still have a choice: they can refuse to walk alongside their human, but then they will be dragged along, even scolded, and there will be no treats. Alternatively, a dog can walk along the set path – frightening buckets and all – and receive both praise and treats from their human at the end. Our choices and actions are still ours to make, but the path is followed in either case.

We must therefore see things as they are, and accept them as part of the wider meaning or Logos of the universe. It follows that we must accept whatever fate has in store for us, however unpleasant it may appear. Some dogs, Barkus acknowledged, may find this challenging, and to them the *Meditations* offers this good advice:

When you wake up in the morning, tell yourself: the people I deal with today may be overbearing, surly, and strict; they may sit around watching TV instead of rubbing my belly and enjoying the world; they may bake delicious cookies and not give me a single one; they may allow the vacuum cleaner to visit despite my protestations. But, remember, they only behave like this because, like cats, humans can't tell good from evil. But I have

seen the beauty of good and the ugliness
of evil and have recognised no one can
implicate me in its ugliness. Nor can I feel
angry at my human, or hate him. We were
born to work together like leashes and collars,
bellies and belly rubs, food and bowls; like
walkies and fun.

With this in mind, Barkus insisted that happiness
can be found at all times and in all places,
reminding his canine companions, 'Very little is
needed to make you wag your tail; it is all within
yourself in your way of thinking.'

Related topics: Stoicism, ancient Rome, genitals

René Descartes

'If you would be a real seeker after truth, as well as tennis balls, it is necessary that at least once in your life you doubt, as far as possible, all things.'

Name: René Descartes
Dog's name: Renée DesBarkes
Breed: papillon
Born: 1596
Went to live on the farm: 1650
Age in dog years: 229

Principles
- It is impossible to know whether you are really chasing squirrels or just dreaming about chasing squirrels.
- Live each day as though there is an evil, all-powerful cat trying to deceive you.

Likes/favourite pastimes
- Fetching tennis balls, both real and imaginary
- Eating all the good books bequeathed to posterity by other good dogs

Special interest: using mathematical equations to prove that the greater number of bones there are in existence, the greater happiness there will be for any given dog

Impact on philosophy

You are on your walkies. You are off the lead. You find yourself in the middle of some pleasant woods. Then, in the corner of your eye, you spot it: the squirrel. Naturally, you give chase. The squirrel is fast and sneaky, but you have the blood of wolves in your veins. Centuries of inbreeding have turned you into a sleek, mean, squirrel-catching machine (compare: human aristocrats). You watch the squirrel's bushy tail draw near. Its scent flares in your nostrils. You are gaining on it. You almost have it in your jaws, and then...

You wake up suddenly, spring from your bed where you were dreaming, and run head first into a door. You look around. There are no squirrels in sight, but humans just happen to have filmed the whole thing on their camera phones, and now one's uploading it to YouTube. Ashamed, you limp out into the garden, tail between your legs, and contemplate what this all means.

Dogs everywhere will have experienced a similar scenario at some point in their lives. And, for one philosophically minded canine, it was just such a 'false awakening' that helped found an entire school of canine philosophy.

This canine was, of course, Renée DesBarkes – a French papillon who barked loudly and often during the early seventeenth century. After having a (very good) dream about catching a whole scurry of squirrels, DesBarkes awoke to discover that she was still indoors and had simply eaten her human master's lecture notes. Later, this gave the human, Descartes, the opportunity to claim that a dog had eaten his homework,* but in the short term the whole sorry episode simply left DesBarkes being called a bad dog, and she was forced to ask herself some deep, at times troubling, questions.

The first was simple. As we go about and live our lives, can we ever be sure we're not dreaming? Some of the dreams we have are obviously fantastic; they could never occur in the real world (for instance, dreams in which cats appear as anything other than the demons they really are), but some of our dreams are so realistic it is impossible to tell the difference between dream and reality. And if we cannot tell the difference for sure, or get confused, how can we ever have complete confidence in the physical, literal reality of the food in our bowls, the collars on our necks or the sticks that we fetch?

DesBarkes determined that it would be worth trying to work out what – if anything – one could know for certain. She hoped this would increase the number of *real* squirrels she was able to catch, and decrease (hopefully to zero) the number of times she was called a bad dog. To do this, she invented what is now known as the method of Barkesian doubt. It is easy enough for dogs to follow the method. All it means is that one must not accept anything as true if there is the slightest possibility that it isn't.

As an example, think of a walk on which you

come across a number of discarded apples. There are no humans around, and the apples would just go to waste if you didn't eat them. However, you have been caught out before by apples, some of which were rotten and mouldy, and gave you the emergency poops all over the human's Afghan rug. Because of these bad apples, you had to see the vet, who seemed to jab you extra hard with his needle, perhaps because you pooped all over him too.

So, you need to be sure the apples are good, and that there isn't a bad apple among them. How would you go about determining this? One way would be to take the time to sniff and inspect each of the apples, one by one, and to put all the suspect fruit to one side, leaving them for the wasps. You might then accidentally ignore a couple of good apples (ones that are only a bit off), but the happy result would be that only definitely, absolutely good apples would make it into your belly.

This is the Barkesian method of doubt in practice. You take a belief such as 'I am chasing squirrels right now' and examine it, and you only accept it as being true if you are certain it can't be wrong or misleading. If there is even the tiniest room for doubt, you must reject it, just like you rejected those possibly rotten, probably delicious apples.

Of course, DesBarkes acknowledged that, should you ever *really* happen on a whole load of discarded apples, then it is probably for the best

---

* It also led the human philosopher to argue that dogs did not have souls. Of course, he had to do this in order to cover his tracks – to justify stealing canine ideas. Descartes committed other unspeakable acts against dog-kind, even against his own pup, and this is one of the reasons he remains, to this day, one of philosophy's most notorious 'puplick' enemies.

that you eat them all anyway, just to be completely sure you haven't missed something lovely. After all, there's a chance you might be dreaming, in which case you've nothing to worry about. There will be no emergency poops on expensive rugs, and no trips to the vet (unless you're having a nightmare).

Urging her canine companions to remain sceptical of reality, so as to catch a glimpse of certain truth, DesBarkes woofed, 'If you would be a real seeker after truth, as well as tennis balls, it is necessary that at least once in your life you doubt, as far as possible, all things.'

In her quest for certainty, DesBarkes ironically provided dogs with more reasons to doubt things than reasons to be sure of them. From her evaluation of dreams, she began to seek out pieces of concrete evidence she knew could be relied on to help her distinguish reality from the world of the imagination. She began by thinking first about the evidence that comes to us through our senses: through seeing, touching, smelling, tasting and hearing.

Can we trust our senses? How can we be sure that, when we see both colours of the rainbow, other dogs, or beings, see the same colours? Perhaps humans see multiple colours! This seems intuitively a ridiculous notion, because we know that humans are more primitive than dogs in every conceivable way. Nevertheless, there are still examples from real life that suggest not all senses are created equal, nor are they equal among different species.

When dogs can hear cats and ghosts many streets away, why is it humans seem only to hear – and care about – the helpful noise a dog makes in response to such dangers? Can we trust our senses? The answer, DesBarkes insisted, was an emphatic no. Emphatically, an emphatic no. Even more emphatic than when the human tells you *not* to eat the Victoria sponge that has been left on the side.

Take the example of a tennis ball, DesBarkes says. The yellow orb of fun may look as though it is in the human's hand, and the human may swing his arm in a way that suggests he has thrown the ball. But how many times have you been led astray by such things? How many times have you given chase to an imaginary ball?

If the answer is ever more than once (and, let us be honest, it is many times more than that), then your sight is not infallible. And, if that's the case, you cannot rely on it for evidence of what is or isn't real. This led DesBarkes to a startling conclusion: think of everything you see as an illusion. She barked, 'I suppose therefore that all things I see are illusions; I believe that no tennis balls have ever existed – ignoring what my lying memory tells me. I think I have no senses. What is there then that can be taken as true? Perhaps only this one thing, that nothing at all is certain.'

DesBarkes also examined mathematical knowledge. We know, don't we, DesBarkes said, that two bones plus two bones will give you a very good day and a very happy dog. We also know, thanks to Pythagoras' dog Linus, that the triangles of our ears have three sides, and will always be soft and good for stroking. Surely, there is nothing to doubt here.

Of course, DesBarkes found plenty of room for doubt, and conducted a famous thought

experiment to make her point. She asked dogs
to imagine the existence of a fiendish devil-cat
who controls everything in the world. Admittedly,
it isn't hard either to imagine such a cat, evil as
felines so clearly are, or to believe it would want
such power. If this devil-cat existed, it could make
it seem that two bones plus two bones equalled
happy dogs and happiness, when *in reality* their
sum might equal *very* happy dogs and *great*
happiness. All this time we might have thought
our ears had three sides, when in reality they have
eight. You wouldn't know the cat was peddling
these illusions; you'd be having your ears stroked
as usual, and everything would seem innocent.
Because the cat is so powerful, there's no way of
proving his nasty tricks aren't happening. Perhaps
the cat is so devilish he's letting you think your
ears are being stroked and your tummy tickled,
when in fact all you are is a doggy brain in a jar.

Once again, DesBarkes has probed our certainties
and found them wanting. But this is not to say
that all of her philosophical barking should
drive you mad with doubt. Quite the opposite
in fact, because one can find certainty through
doubt itself.

'Even if some evil cat is tricking you into thinking
these thoughts, there is something, some "you"
somewhere, that is having these thoughts,'
DesBarkes explained. 'To doubt is to think, and to
think is to exist.'

Therefore, 'Dogito, ergo sum.' I am a dog that
thinks, therefore I am.

Related topics: reality, France, tennis balls

John Locke

*'All dogs by nature are equal, in
that equal right that every dog
hath to her natural freedom,
without being subjected to the
will or authority of any other
dog – or of any man.'*

Name: John Locke
Dog's name: John Licke
Breed: English springer spaniel
Born: 1632
Went to live on the farm: 1704
Age in dog years: 301

Principles
- All dogs are created equal.
- If a dog cannot remember doing something
  'naughty', it cannot – indeed must not –
  be punished.

Likes/favourite pastimes
- Eating socks
- Hanging out under apple trees with Isaac
  Newton's dog

Special interest: toleration for the beliefs of all
dogs and humans

Impact on philosophy

'What were you like as a puppy?' This is one of
the main questions that English philosopher's
dog John Licke poses to canines everywhere.
Licke believed that our understanding of the
world comes only through experience, and so, as
newborn pups, our minds are a *tabula rasa* – a
blank slate, or a bowl with no kibble in it. Our
minds might be able to think and reason, but they
possess no ideas – no consciousness. This is why,
he reasoned, dogs must be taught to do tricks, to
sit or stay.

This way of thinking had certain implications
for Licke's philosophy that went beyond the
psychological analysis of puppies (even the very
cute ones). Licke noticed that most dogs can't
remember what it was like to be a puppy. We
change over time, growing and developing,
eventually turning grey around the muzzle. We
learn and forget things, leave behind the friends
whose bottoms we sniff, make new friends, sniff
new bottoms and prioritise different things. If
this is the case, in what sense are old and young
versions of a dog the same animal?

Licke saw that this was a problem that didn't just
apply to dogs and puppies, or even human beings.
Take a pair of socks, he said.

> You may, in your daily investigations, come
> across a tasty-looking pair of socks that
> your human has left invitingly on the floor.
> It would be rude not to take a bite or two.

Now, because humans are often foolish and mean-minded, they may see what you have done, take the socks and repair them, stitching on new pieces of fabric. A few days later, you find these mended socks once again and rightly try to teach your human a lesson in philosophy by eating the remaining bits of original sock. So that, when the human mends the socks for a second time, all of the original material is replaced. In what sense, therefore, are these mended socks still the original socks?

Licke's way of answering this question was to point out that, while fur may fall out, regrow and turn grey, and while a good boy's balls may be chopped off and a good girl spayed, we are living things and so, biologically, the same as we ever were. But, Licke insisted, there is an important difference between being the same animal, and being the same *dog*.

According to Licke, we can be the same canine, but not the same dog as previously, because our consciousness develops and changes over time – from that blank bowl-of-mind devoid of even the tiniest morsel, to one stacked with heaps of tasty treats.

'A dog's personal identity', he barked, 'depends on consciousness, not substance.'

To illustrate his point, he described a scenario in which two dogs, belonging to a prince and a cobbler respectively, switch memories. The prince's dog, used to a life spent eating roast swan and sleeping on the softest silken dog bed, wakes to find himself in a dusty workshop where there are no swans and lots of rats. The cobbler's dog, accustomed to high praise for killing rats and to being given scraps of tasty shoe leather in return, finds suddenly he is being told off for eating the delicious shoes he unearths in his new, palatial lodgings. According to Licke, consciousness determines which dog is which: if you have the memory of a prince's dog, that is who you are; if you remember the workshop and leather, you are the cobbler's dog, even if you now possess the body of a royal hound.

For Licke, matters of consciousness were closely tied to matters of personal responsibility. If a dog could not remember doing something 'wrong' – like eating a young child's birthday cake and being sick all over the child – it would still be a 'good' dog, and would hardly deserve punishment for a crime of which it had no recollection.

Many dogs have embraced this way of thinking, and that is why they do not look embarrassed after eating your mortgage documents or pooping in your bed, but wag their tails and tilt their heads in confusion as you point and scream and stamp your feet. Why should *they* be punished? With no memory of the incident in question, how can they admit the justice of punishment?

Of course, this wasn't Licke's only contribution to philosophical thought. An English springer spaniel, he was forced to take refuge in the Netherlands after being accused of plotting against King Charles spaniels – many of which happened to be owned by King Charles II. From the continent, he argued for canine-to-canine

toleration, arguing that all dogs are created
equal and have a right to live their lives, eat their
treats and bury their bones wherever they see
fit. His view that we have a dog-given right to
life, happiness and the ownership of the bones
we have buried influenced the founding puppers
of the United States of America. Those dogs
familiar with chewing early drafts of the American
constitution may be familiar with one of Licke's
more famous woofs: 'All dogs by nature are
equal, in that equal right that every dog hath to
her natural freedom, without being subjected to
the will or authority of any other dog – or of any
man... Who is a man to tell any dog what it can or
cannot eat?'

Related topics: empiricism, consciousness,
spaniels, socks

Voltaire

'The mirror is a worthless invention. The only way to truly see yourself is in the reflection of the eyes of someone you love.'

Name: Voltaire
Dog's name: Fur-ançois-Marie Awoooo-et, aka Vol-terrier
Breed: dachshund
Born: 1694
Went to live on the farm: 1778
Age in dog years: 345

Principles
- One must be tolerant of all dogs and their smells.
- Putting blind faith in the commands of humans in authority is absurd.
- You should cherish those who seek bones, but beware those who find them.

Likes/favourite pastimes
- 'Cultivating' gardens by digging up rose bushes
- Rescuing downtrodden dogs from illegal – and immoral – bathtimes

Special interest: freedom of woofs

Impact on philosophy
'If dogs had not existed, it would have been necessary to invent them.' So woofed philosophical French pupper, Fur-ançois-Marie Awooo-et (known more commonly as Vol-terrier). An exceedingly well-trained pooch, Vol-terrier was celebrated across Europe for his witty barks and growls. Yet he also made a habit of saying – and doing – controversial things, such as digging up – or, in his own word, 'cultivating' – people's gardens.

By the standards of eighteenth-century Catholic France, such actions were enough to get anyone in hot water, and Vol-terrier, like all dogs, hated a warm sudsy bath with the passion of a thousand suns. Indeed, the original copy of his *Treatise of Tolerance*, subsequently bastardised by his human 'owner', argued fervently that humans should be more tolerant of 'evil-smelling' dogs. 'It is clear,' he woofed, 'that the man who bathes a dog because he is not of the same scent, is a monster.'

His *Treatise* was inspired by the trial-by-bath of a dog called Jean Collars. Wrongly accused of rolling in fox poop, Collars was bathed without due process in a largely cat-ruled part of Toulouse. In the non-human original *Treatise*, one section paw-fectly illustrates Vol-terrier's argument for tolerance: 'There are about forty millions of dogs in Europe who have not had a bath today; should we say to every one of them, "Hello, dog. Since you are damnably smelly, I shall neither pet, converse with, tickle, play, nor have any connections with you?"'

Such an idea is patently absurd – one should pet and play with all dogs, regardless of odour. But, at the time he was barking, such liberal ideas were scandalous, and Vol-terrier was forced to spend some years of his life in exile in England. There he was introduced to English Enlightenment canines like Diamond, the pooch owned by Isaac Newton, as well as John Licke (whom we met and petted on page 37). Vol-terrier was fascinated by Licke's ideas of canine liberty and by the hard empirical science of Diamond – later framed by her 'owner' and accused of setting fire to his lab notes. (It was Newton, of course, who set fire to Diamond's work, having first made copies in his own hand. Classic man-oeuvre).

Vol-terrier embraced the Enlightenment ideas of his four-legged comrades and used them to support his own liberal philosophy. When he returned to France, he set about challenging the irrational superstitions of humans, taking issue with unnecessary bathing, and refuting the wild claim that you should be fed only *once* a day, and always at the same time. These superstitions, he argued, were being used by humans – and their ultimate duplicitous masters, cats – to maintain power and their sway over several European countries.

As one might expect, such ideas continued to get him in trouble with the authorities, and at one point he had to spend some time in the doghouse – or the Bastille, as humans called it – after growling in an insulting fashion at a French aristo-cat.

Undeterred, Vol-terrier continued to question authority for the rest his life, interrogating the world around him and how people – and dogs – lived within it. Perhaps speaking from experience, he once op-whined, 'It is dangerous to be right in matters on which the established authorities are wrong.'

To many canine students, such ideas can be baffling, and especially to those who have complete faith in their humans. Yet for Vol-terrier, challenging authority and thinking for oneself were essential activities. According to Vol-terrier, a dog that sits only because he is told to may be obedient, but he is not necessarily 'good'. A good dog, by Vol-terrier's standards, *chooses* to sit – and is never forced to do so by some pushy human's hand.

Canine liberalism, then, is ultimately about freedom. Dogs should be free to sit or stand, to roll in fox poop or even eat the fox poop, should they so wish. And they should then be free to lick the faces of their humans, in order to express their happiness at having just eaten poop. At the same time, freedom must be extended to others, and so Vol-terrier stressed it was important that no human be forced to roll in, or eat, poop themselves, even if a dog might – rightly – think them mad for passing up the opportunity.

It was a controversial idea at the time Vol-terrier was barking it. But events have proved its worth. Even today, there are dogs (and humans) without the freedoms enjoyed by others, who are still being persecuted, bathed unnecessarily, forced to sit in one place day in, day out, and denied the treats they can so clearly see others eating. Vol-terrier embraced both controversy and difference of opinion; in the end, his work was about tolerance: tolerance of others' ideas as well as your own. As he is (wrongly) supposed to have woofed, 'I disagree with your decision to give me a bath; but I will defend to the death your right to bathe me.'

Like all the best stories of good dogs, Vol-terrier's tale has a happy ending. In the years before he went to live on the farm, he moved with his 'owner' into a lovely château outside Geneva, in a place called Fur-ney. Vol-terrier's principled forbearance meant he was really very forgiving when he learned that his master had started to publish his barkings under his own name. In response, he famously woofed, 'What a fuss, when you can just eat a tasty omelette!' thereby reminding his followers that genuine enlightenment only comes about in the presence of that most canine of emotions: love. Before leaving to spend more time 'cultivating' the château's extensive rose gardens, Awooo-et barked, 'The mirror is a worthless invention. The only way to truly see yourself is reflected in the eyes of someone you love.'

Related topics: liberalism, tolerance, bathtime

Adam Smith

'Man is an animal who makes foolish bargains. No other animal does this – no dog exchanges bones with another. Why would you ever give your bone away?'

Name: Adam Smith
Dog's name: Adam Sniff
Breed: Coton de Tulear
Born: 1723
Went to live on the farm: 1790
Age in dog years: 281

Principles
- A dog should be left, as though on an invisible leash, to pursue its own self-interest, and in so doing promote the interests of all canine-kind.
- Human government is set up to defend the bone-rich humans against bone-poor dogs, or those who have some bones against those who have none at all.
- No pack of dogs can be flourishing and happy if the greater part of its number does not have bones or does not receive sufficient belly rubs.

Likes/favourite pastimes
- Burying bones and forgetting where said bones are buried
- Touring France on long walkies with the dogs of young French aristocrats

Special interest: studying how bones are earned, how they are used, buried or eaten, and which dogs receive the most bones for doing what

Impact on philosophy
It is a truth universally acknowledged (by dogs) that only humans are foolish enough to have come up with the idea of a thing like money. It's useless for playing fetch (the notes can't be thrown and the metal discs just get lost in the grass) and it's very painful to poop out.

But this is not to say that dogs lack their own means of exchange. Canines tend to trade in the currencies of praise, exciting sticks, tasty bones and sniffed bottoms – a varied system largely overlooked by canine philosophers until the advent of a very clever pup called Adam Sniff, born in Scotland in the mid-eighteenth century.

Sniff went to Glasgow university as a young pup, where tutors were quick to praise his sharp mind and ability to use his nose to track down and make off with delicious half-cooked steaks before college chefs noticed anything. On account of both his intelligence and exceptionally boop-able nose, Sniff was awarded a smell scholarship (still in existence today) to study various intriguing scents in and around Balliol College, Oxford.

Sniff would become an academic philosopher, writing a major book about the importance of being sympathetic to dogs who are not currently receiving belly rubs, and lecturing regularly on the importance of providing all dogs with as many rubs as possible.

It would be a surprise to Sniff, therefore, that his ideas – in purloined human form – are considered to have laid the foundations of modern economics. He would find it odd, not least because, for Sniff, humans were always a puzzle, creatures who never knew quite what to do with things of real value. He once woofed, 'Man is an animal who makes foolish bargains. No other animal does this – no dog exchanges bones with another. Why would you ever give your bone away?'

These questions interested Sniff, in part because he was perplexed by the way rich humans flaunt their possessions and wealth. For Sniff, display was not only garish and unnecessary (If you had so much money, why weren't you buying more food for dogs who can't afford it?) but wholly illogical. Surely, he argued, if you had something of value, like a delicious bone, you would want to hide it and protect it from others, not show it off.

These notions ultimately led Sniff to develop a radically fresh understanding of how canine societies work. He argued that social harmony will emerge naturally if dogs are allowed to live and work together, going wherever they please and wandering about as if on an invisible, infinitely extendable lead.

He barked,

> By preferring to take his bones and bury them, one by one, in a well-hidden place, that he may shortly forget the location of,

the dog intends only his own gain, and is led *as though on an invisible lead* to promote an end which was no part of his intention. By this we mean that though his original intention may have been to hide the bones, the inevitable forgetting of their location will likely mean another dog will shortly be along to uncover them – bringing great enjoyment as the new dog, in turn, looks for a place to bury the bones and subsequently forget all about them. The invisible lead is a vital part of any functioning canine society – and most dogs will never notice its presence. By being allowed to pursue its own interests, each individual dog, in turn, promotes the interests of canine society at large.

In Sniff's view, a prospering canine order does not need to be controlled by humans – or physical leashes. It will grow, organically, as a product of canine nature. It will grow best in an open park or playing field, with free exchange of Frisbees and large sticks, and without demands placed on dogs by humans to 'Sit,' 'Stay' or 'Stop eating that.'

The Woofs of Nations was therefore not just a study of what would become known as snacknomics (the economics of things that can be eaten), but a survey of canine social psychology: a reflection on life, welfare (or well-fur), bones and morality (and bones again, just for good measure).

Related topics: economics, the invisible lead, bones

Immanuel Kant

'They ask me who is a "good" dog, but what can I know? I cannot ever know enough to accurately ascertain what "goodness" even means. Still, all I may hope is that there are good dogs, that I may keep faith in the goodness of dogs and the progress of canines everywhere.'

Name: Immanuel Kant
Dog's name: Immanu-howl Kant
Breed: greyhound
Born: 1724
Went to live on the farm: 1804
Age in dog years: 333

Principles
- A good dog is a moral dog.
- A dog must act as though their every action could become a universal law.
- Act so as to treat dogs and people always as ends in themselves, never as mere means.

Likes/favourite pastimes
- Highly regimented walkies taken at 4.30 p.m. precisely every day

Special interest: exploring the difference between an analytic proposition ('All cats are evil') and a synthetic one ('All food is delicious'). While analytic propositions are true by definition (a cat is evil by its very nature), synthetic propositions require investigation to determine their veracity. It is a dog's duty to investigate all sources of food to check whether the food is delicious. Kant was known to investigate potential sources of food with rigorous – if orderly – gusto.

Impact on philosophy
'What if every dog did that?'

This is the question that one of the most influential philosophers' dogs instructed all canines to consider before taking any action.

Immanu-howl Kant was obsessed with what it meant to be 'good' ever since his master asked him, 'Who's a good dog, then?' while he was a puppy. Intrigued by the question, Kant was left unconvinced by his human's insistence that he – Immanu-howl – was indeed a good boy (actually a very, *very* good boy, apparently); after all, what evidence did his human have to back up this assertion?

For Kant, goodness was something that could be achieved, and deduced, through logical reasoning. One cannot be a good dog simply because a human tells you that you are; to prove such an assertion, you need to investigate further, observing your behaviour and seeing whether or not it follows what Kant described as 'universal laws'.

Unlike instructions given by fallible humans – 'Sit,' 'Stay,' 'Stop humping that cushion' – a universal law is something that should be followed because it is the right thing to do, and it is what every dog in the same situation should do.

Consider the following situation. You're out in the garden beside your kennel, minding your own business. Perhaps you have just successfully slain another dangerous foe in the form of a squeaky pink elephant, or maybe you are closer than ever to catching your own tail. All of a sudden, your best dog-friend from next door bursts through your fence with a large roast turkey in her mouth. She drops it at your feet and breathlessly explains that she has stolen the turkey from her human, who is now very angry and looking for her. You tell her to hide in your kennel, and she duly disappears inside – along with the turkey. Moments later, her human crashes through the same fence and stares at you. He is holding a large carving knife and does not look pleased. He asks you where your friend is. Is she here? Where is the turkey? You know she is in your doghouse, but you tell a lie. You bark happily at the human and show him your defeated squeaky toy. You indicate with your nose that your friend is probably in the park. The human stalks away.

Surely, in this scenario, you have done the right thing by sending the angry human away from your friend. He had a big knife and everything. Perhaps you have saved her life! Certainly, you have saved her a great deal of trouble. What's more, the two of you now have a delicious turkey all to yourselves. This must have been a moral act, mustn't it?

Not according to Kant. Kant thought you should *never* lie. And you shouldn't steal food that belongs to humans either, not even the most delicious roast turkey. You may have acted as you did because you thought that, by protecting your friend, you might enjoy a piece of turkey, and Kant felt strongly that you should never do anything simply for the possibility, or promise, of reward. The truly moral act would have been to tell the truth, even though that might have put at risk your friend's safety and freedom. There are no exceptions or excuses to this rule, Kant says. You cannot make a universal law out of the principle of expedience – that everyone should lie when it best suits them, or that everyone should steal food when hungry.

This is why, Kant howled, dogs need to ask themselves, 'What if every dog did that?' before taking action. Consider: if dogs took and ate all the turkeys, the humans in their malnourished state might be unable to give belly rubs. And what sort of world would that be?

This way of thinking about 'right' and 'wrong', and the actions that define a 'good' dog is based on cool reasoning and logic. As you may have guessed, Kant, like his philosophy, was very ordered and logical, so much so that he imposed a strict pattern on each day. In order not to waste time, he would howl loudly from 5 a.m. sharp in order to wake his 'master' (hence the name, Immanu-howl). He would then drink cold tea from his water bowl, lick his balls while his master smoked a tobacco pipe (Immanu-howl thought the former activity 'much more delicious and healthy') and begin work.

He was an extremely productive dog, burying several of his masters' books in various spots around the yard, and receiving an extremely high number of head strokes and chin tickles from students at the local university.

At 4.30 p.m. sharp he took his master for daily walkies. Together they passed up and down the street eight times. It was such a precise routine that the residents of Konigsberg could set their watches by the sight of Immanu-howl's wagging tail.

Such an ordered and logical life might seem absurd, yet for Kant all things were undertaken in pursuit of something higher: pure reason. He once barked, 'All our knowledge begins with the senses. Does that cowpat smell delicious? Yes. Does it taste delicious? Also, yes. From there, we can proceed to the understanding that cowpats *are* delicious. Finally, knowledge ends with reason – the reason we eat the cowpat is because it is delicious. There is nothing higher than reason.'

His dedication to reason and morality is Immanu-howl's great contribution to canine philosophy. By Kant's own logic, his human 'owner' took actions that one must consider immoral: stealing your dog's ideas can never become a universal law. But it is also true that his human got one very important thing right: Immanu-howl Kant was a very good dog, oh yes he was, yes he was. Even if he didn't know it.

Related topics: reason, morality, turkey

51

Mary Wollstonecraft

'I do not wish for dogs to have power over humans, but over themselves.'

Name: Mary Wollstonecraft
Dog's name: Ms Woof-stonecraft
Breed: Yorkshire terrier
Born: 1759
Went to live on the farm: 1797
Age in dog years: 266

Principles
- There are good girls as well as good boys.
- You must give female dogs the same training as you provide to their male counterparts, so that everyone can catch the same Frisbee.

Likes/favourite pastimes
- Supporting the overthrow of the French ruling aristo-cats
- Chewing over the written words of other progressive thinkers and writers

Special interest: making sure she has eaten the same number of delicious cookies as her male dog counterparts

Impact on philosophy

In much of this book so far, we've shown how *men* have passed off their dogs' ideas as philosophical innovations of their own. But, right now, spare a thought for all the female dogs owned by female philosophers, who couldn't even have their ideas stolen and published by their 'owners' thanks to centuries of patriarchal oppression. Indeed, of all the crimes committed against canine-kind by man, there is arguably none so egregious as the suppression – by men – of the ideas of female dogs (and their humans).

One dog who sought to change this was the Yorkshire terrier 'owned' by human writer and 'philosopher' Mary Wollstonecraft. Ms Woof-stonecraft was frustrated that the playing fields of philosophy were dominated by males (dogs or otherwise), leaving female doggies hardly any space to play and precious few fresh cowpats to roll in. She vociferously disputed the views held by some of her contemporaries – like Jean Jack-Russell – that female dogs should be trained only for the pleasure of men.

In a heated debate in the park, in which not a single bottom was sniffed, Ms Woof-stonecraft called on Jack-Russell to justify his logic, asking, 'If dogs be trained for dependence – that is, to act according to the will of another fallible being – and submit, right or wrong, to power, where are we to stop?'

Woof-stonecraft argued that, having been denied the same training as their male counterparts, lady dogs had been turned into 'toys' for men. This she found particularly hard to stomach, given there were never any toys available for lady dogs to play with. She also took umbrage at the language used by humans to praise canine-kind for performing dutiful actions, once barking, 'Everybody always assumes you're a good boy, but sometimes you're a good girl.'

The idea that girls could be good dogs too certainly ruffled some fur and led to more than one head tilted in curiosity. Woof-stonecraft's line of thinking was pretty unconventional in eighteenth-century canine circles. And especially so in England – a land in which the dog parks were dominated by a certain kind of upper-class English bulldog, who could barely breathe thanks to centuries of inbreeding. But, then again, Woof-stonecraft was a pretty unconventional kind of dog.

On her various daring and adventurous walkies, she got caught up chasing – and overthrowing – the ruling aristo-cats in the French Revolution, met and fell in love with the dog of an American adventurer and fell in with a group of radical poetical dogs including William Bark and William Wordswoof, whose lyrical woofs were later stolen by their humans, Blake and Wordsworth.

While living in Bath, Woof-stonecraft was further radicalised when told, on her arrival at the world-famous Roman bathhouses, that dogs were not permitted in the baths – not even to chase or bark at the suspicious seagulls floating about on the water. Infuriated at the limited options available to female dogs, she left Bath and set up a school for girl puppies, where she sought to provide a level of training equal to that received by their male counterparts.

These experiences all fed into her most important literary contribution to female-canine liberation: *A Vindication of the Rights of Bitches*. In this brilliant essay she argued forcefully for dogs as being vital to their country as educators of people (Is there anyone who has not learned something from their dog?) and for strict equality of training, barking, 'Contending for the rights of women, my main argument is built on this simple principle, that lessons in how to catch Frisbees must be taught to all, or else no Frisbees will ever be caught well.'

She urged dogs to think rationally and not be slaves to sense or sensibility. They should control their instincts, even when picking up the scent of the mischievous badger from next door. By allowing reason and feeling to work in tandem, dogs could then be of the utmost value and help 'refine civilisation'.

'Strengthen the canine mind by enlarging it,' she urged, 'and there will be an end to blind obedience – dogs should not sit simply because they are told to do so, but because they choose to ... Make [bitches] rational creatures and free from the leash, and they will quickly become good dogs – that is, if humans do not neglect their duties as good companions.'

Crucially, Woof-stonecraft encouraged her 'owner', Mary, to fight for equal rights for human women too. She did this by clawing at the front door until walkies finally began, and then proceeding to pull

Mary down to meetings and gatherings of the early feminist movement. She recognised, pragmatically, that until female humans were treated as equals with their male counterparts, her own ideas might be dismissed and ignored.

Woof-stonecraft's passionate radicalism threw the metaphorical tennis ball and got it rolling for future feminist philosophers. Until she came along, the ball had been firmly stuck in the grass, and no amount of barking or jumping nearby had freed it. In this way, she was a true tailblazer and remains a doggy icon to all canine-rights puppers to this day.

Related topics: feminism, equality, Frisbees

Søren Kierkegaard

'Meaning only truly comes from returning the ball. But this requires that the ball be first thrown.'

Name: Søren Kierkegaard
Dog's name: Søren Kierkegrrrr
Breed: husky
Born: 1813
Went to live on the farm: 1855
Age in dog years: 181

Principles
- Walkies are the route to well-being.
- The ball must be returned, but first it must be thrown.
- The anxiety of being separated from your human is real but necessary.

Likes/favourite pastimes
- Eating abandoned smorgasbord
- Long howling matches with Whine-elm Heel-girl, the dog 'owned' by Wilhelm Hegel

Special interest: taking a leap of faith into the arms of a good human for cuddles

Impact on philosophy

As dog philosophy was stolen and shaped by dogs' 'owners' over the centuries, new strands of revolutionary thought emerged, philosophies that sought not merely to provide guidelines on how to be a virtuous or 'good' dog, but instead tried to critique the fundamental nature of existence. Why do we wag our tails? How can we be true to ourselves, while also being part of a pack? Is it possible to reconcile truth with the existence of cats?

The proponents of these new ways of thinking were often thought of as being barking mad – and none more so than Danish philosophical pupper, Søren Kierkegrrrr. Often mocked by his litter mates for his spindly legs and pointy fur, Kierkegrrrr was known for taking long, daily walks about the streets of Copenhagen.

Just as Aristotle's dog extolled the virtues of peripatetic philosophy, so Kierkegrrrr noted that it was through the act of walkies that one maintained one's physical and mental health, advanced philosophy and had one's best thoughts. After one walk on which he discovered not one but *two* delicious slices of stale bread foolishly discarded by a human, Kierkegrrrr growled, 'No matter what happens, do not lose your desire to go for walkies: every day I walk myself into a state of well-being and walk away from every illness; I have walked myself into my best thoughts, and I know of no thought so burdensome that one cannot walk away from it.'

Similar benefits might be derived from wagging your tail, Kierkegrrrr argued, as well as participating in wholesome activities with your human, such as stick-catching, squirrel-chasing, or trying to teach humans not to throw their balls away.

This line of argument ruffled a good deal of fur in bottom-sniffing circles. Among Kierkegrrrr's canine comrades, Whine-elm Heel-girl bemoaned humans' seeming inability to keep hold of their balls, arguing that there was no logic in forever retrieving that which they seemed intent on losing. Kierkegrrrr disagreed vehemently, arguing that the process of fetching a thrown ball was the perfect metaphor for understanding life: you can only return a ball if it has been thrown, just as you may only understand life once it has been lived. To this end, he barked, 'Meaning only truly comes from returning the ball. But this requires that the ball be first thrown.'

This disagreement started a war of woofs and long howls between the two philosophers' dogs that would lead to many complaints from the neighbours.

Like many dogs, Kierkegrrrr took issue with the establishment cat class. Cats, he argued, never wanted revolutionary change. They were content with the status quo, with being waited on hand-on-paw and allowed to come and go as they pleased without giving anything back apart from heavy-lidded looks of disdain and messy litter trays. They'd never wanted dogs or humans to think for themselves; it wasn't in their interests. But, said Kierkegrrrr,

I want dogs to sit up and take notice; I want to prevent them from idling away and wasting their lives. Cats take it for granted that a lot of people will always go to waste. But they keep silent about it; they live sheltered lives pretending that all these many, many people simply do not exist. That is what is ungodly about the superior status of cats; in order to be comfortable themselves, they do not even call attention to anything.

For all Kierkegrrrr's passion for walkies and fetch, and the persuasiveness of his laments against feline-kind, perhaps his greatest contribution to canine philosophy was his articulation of the anxiety so many dogs feel when their human leaves them alone in the house.

Noting the confusion and torment that arises in every dog's soul when abandoned by their human, Kierkegrrrr described a feeling of 'angst' that arises from the fear of being left alone for an indeterminate amount of time (hours or months – impossible to tell) and the conflictual urge either to chase after the human (to end the separation) or 'Stay' as instructed, and be called a 'good dog' should the human return. This experience is one of anxiety or dread because of our complete freedom to choose either to leave or stay put. The fact that there exists the possibility of doing something is deeply entwined with the fact that one has the freedom to do it, and this is enough to trigger immense feelings of terror that may cause one to widdle on the floor or chew correspondence. Kierkegrrrr called this our 'dizziness of freedom' – a sensation not dissimilar to chasing one's tail in circles once too often. In one searing diatribe

Kierkegrrrr summed up the dilemma as follows: 'Chase after your human and you will regret it. Stay alone in the house instead and you will regret that too. Eat the food and you will regret it; don't eat the food and you will regret it. Whether you chase the cat or don't chase the cat, you will regret it. This, doggos, is the essence of all philosophy.'

Discussing what reaction a dog could logically take in response to such anxiety-inducing experiences, Kierkegrrrr noted, 'Anxiety can just as well express itself by muteness as by a howl.'

Everywhere he turned, Kierkgrrrr saw incompatibilities and impossible choices (and quite often the end of his tail, always disappearing while being so close).

> Any dog who has given the matter any serious thought will know that I am right when I say it is not possible for any pup to be absolutely and completely content, not even for a single half-hour of its life. No dog has ever been left alone in the house without crying. Humans never ask you if you are OK with them leaving (you are not), and they won't tell you how long they have been away (if, and when, they return), nor will they tell you when they will next abandon you. You can eat all of their post and all of their loo roll. You can poop in their kitchen and in their bed. You can find their bag of couscous in the cupboard and eat it all, but it will not bring back the humans, and it will only fill you with regret (and couscous). When the humans return, they may say it has only been three score and ten minutes, but really, how

can we know? It may well have been weeks, months, or even years.

To overcome this existential anxiety, Søren suggested, each and every dog needed to take a dramatic 'leap of faith'. This concept acknowledged the reality that, in being abandoned by its human, a dog is faced with a choice that cannot be justified rationally – you must believe the human will return, even though you have no way of knowing they will – and into which the dog must therefore 'leap'.

In a nod to his stoical philosophical litter mates, Kierkegrrrr noted that anxiety is 'an adventure that every dog must go through – to learn to be anxious in order that he may not become a bad dog either by never having been in a state of anxiety or by succumbing to anxiety'. He insisted, 'Never cease loving a person, and never give up hope for their return.'

Related topics: anxiety, faith, tennis balls

Karl Marx

> *'Canines of the world, unite!*
> *You have nothing to lose but*
> *your leashes.'*

Name: Karl Marx
Dog's name: Karl Barks
Breed: German schnauzer
Born: 1818
Went to live on the farm: 1883
Age in dog years: 313

Principles:
- The history of all canine culture is the struggle for an equal share of treats.
- Dogs control the means of walkies.
- Cats are a bourgeois construct.

Likes/favourite pastimes
- Seizing the means of production of dog food
- The emancipation of all canines – especially working dogs – from capitalist power structures, like veterinary clinics
- Arranging butt-sniffing politburos with other dogs while out in the park

Special interest: urinating on private property

Impact on philosophy
Perhaps one of the most influential figures in human history, Karl Marx – like all bourgeois humans – achieved fame and notoriety by nicking his dog's best ideas.

Raised a bushily bearded pup in the Prussian town of Trier on the Lower Rhine, Barks held that all societies develop through the struggle between different classes of both humans and dogs. In achieving this insight, he was inspired by his neighbour's dog, Friedrich Beagles, and by his own daily struggle with the postman for the letters and parcels that Beagles saw as his. After one particularly violent tussle for a parcel containing some of the finest capitalist chocolate, Barks noted that the only way to establish parity between the rule of the postman and the suppression of the canine would be through the violent overthrow of existing power structures.

Employing a critical approach known as historical materialism, Barks predicted that, as in earlier socio-economic systems and relationships, the delivery and control of the post by humans naturally created internal tensions that would lead eventually to systemic collapse and the devouring of said post by dogs unfairly left out of this paradigm.

For Barks, the relationships between post and delivery, or man and dog, were inherently unstable and prone to crisis. Using the example of the Dutch tulip crisis, he pointed out that, while humans believed this financial crash to have been caused by rogue financial speculation, dogs understood that it was really the fault of one rather mischievous Clumber spaniel who got into the delivery warehouse and ate all the bulbs. As these types of events became more frequent, Barks argued, class and canine consciousness would increase, leading at last to a canine assumption of political power and the establishment of a classless and species-agnostic society, in which dogs could eat as many tulip bulbs and chew as many letters and parcels as they pleased. In this system, Barks barked, there would be no need for postal or delivery services at all, as no one would have a fixed address. Instead, everybody would live in their favourite place: the park.

Barks actively pressed for the implementation of such a society, arguing that canines around the world were bound not by their differences but by their similarities; specifically, the fact that they were oppressed by the human bourgeois class. In a number of key addresses to canines he met on various walks, he argued that dogs should carry out organised revolutionary action to topple human power structures and bring about their emancipation from dogs' otherwise human-controlled and -dominated lives.

Central to Barks's thesis was his re-evaluation of canine nature. He argued that canines recognise that they possess both actual and potential selves, but that they only derive meaning from these selves when they can influence their own lives. Under prevailing conditions, as he saw them, Barks perceived this to be impossible as long as dogs were not given control of their lives and destinies. 'In a day when you must wait for your human master to pour the food into your bowl, and then be told to sit, to wait, to stay, before being allowed to eat the food, the canine is only ever told to obey. He is not told to live,' Barks observed. 'Though he eats the food, he does not control the food. It is the same with every aspect of a dog's life. For the dog must wait inside the home, until granted permission to go outdoors for walkies by – once again – the human "owner". Even then, the dog is kept in line, sometimes even physically, on a leash. In this way, the dog has no autonomy – without which the result can only ever be alienation from one's self and from one's destiny.'

Sadly for Barks, he did not live to see his ideas put into practice. After one too many letters in his neighbourhood were eaten, Barks and Beagles were forced to flee their homes along with their 'owners', finding themselves in exile in what in many ways is the proverbial doghouse of Europe, England.

After his death – he was felled by a cricket ball that he may or may not have been chasing – Barks's reputation grew. His ideas would become the governing principles of the dogs taking part in the Bolshevik revolution in Russia in 1917: 'From each according to his ability to eat the food, to each according to his need to eat the food.' The rest is history.

Related topics: dog chains, revolution, walkies

Friedrich Nietzsche

'When you gaze long into the abyss of an empty bowl of food, the empty bowl of food gazes also into you.'

Name: Friedrich Nietzsche
Dog's name: Free-lick
Breed: Hungarian puli
Born: 1844
Went to live on the farm: 1900
Age in dog years: 237

Principles
- Dog is dead.
- We must live our lives in such a way that we would be happy to live them exactly as they have been experienced, over and over again, for ever.
- All dogs are 'super-dogs' – something man can only aspire to be.

Likes/favourite pastimes
- Staring into the abyss of an empty food bowl
- Howling along to Wagner

Special interest: big fan of moustaches

Impact on philosophy
What would the most virtuous being in the universe be like? What traits would it have? For German philosophical pupper Free-lick Nietzsche, the answer was obvious: a virtuous being would be strong and noble, and would live its life by its own rules and truth. In other words, it would be a dog.

Free-lick used the term *Überhunde* – or 'super-dog' – to describe this ideal canine. All dogs have the capacity to be super, he insisted, but many are prevented from fulfilling their potential by their subjection to the rules and constraints placed on them by their 'owners'. Pointing out that, as free dogs and wolves, canines had long roamed the planet, hunting mighty beasts and living in harmony with nature, Free-lick argued that domesticated dogs were effectively enslaved creatures, and had internalised a human notion of the 'good'.

Nietzsche wanted to dispel man-made conceptions of what a dog should be, famously barking, 'Dog is dead.' This caused considerable controversy in the canine world, since it is rude to talk about the death of individual dogs (and inaccurate, since they all live for ever), but Free-lick was undeterred in his beliefs. He became obsessed with the idea of self-creation: that a dog must become who s/he is by creating morality, purpose and meaning in its own life, rather than looking to anybody else to do it for them.

Central to Free-lick's notion of self-creation was the idea of owning one's choices and their consequences. For example, a super-dog might eat all of the human's Easter egg, not because s/he desires it, but because s/he is happy to live with the consequences of that action, even if it means being sent to the doghouse, or called something terrible, like 'bad dog'.

Pointing out that many dogs seem to value praise from a human more than doing something because they truly wish to do it, Free-lick woofed, 'I cannot believe in a dog who wants to be praised all the time. If you desire to sleep in the human's bed, you must do it – perhaps even concealing yourself in the blankets. And do not be afraid to fart at the humans while you sleep beside them. Even if they scold you for letting one off, remember – what does not kill you makes you stronger.'

At the core of Free-lick's philosophy is the idea of the *'eternal return'* – the ultimate embrace of responsibility that comes from accepting the consequences, good or bad, of one's willed action. Embedded in this is a call for dogs to live their lives in such a way that makes the consequences of actions tolerable, so that if they were forced to live their lives again in exactly the same way, for ever, it would be no great hardship.

Free-lick used a thought experiment to illustrate his ideas. He asked dogs to imagine being very old and taken by their humans to live on the farm across the rainbow bridge. There they would be met by a farmer who would tell them that the farm they believed in did not exist; instead, the life they had just lived must be lived again, in exactly the same way.

'There will be nothing new in this life,' Free-lick barked. 'Every pain you experience, when you see a cat or when the human leaves, will remain. Every moment of fear at seeing a vacuum cleaner will be lived once again, but so too will every instance of joy – at the return of your human, or the sight of a full food bowl. Every wag of your tail, every bark, every sigh and breath, everything unspeakably small or great in your life will return to you, all in the same succession and sequence.'

Free-lick's question, or challenge, to dogs everywhere is one that can be answered not in mere woofs but only in the course of life itself: 'The question in each and every thing is, "Do you want to eat this again, and innumerable times again? Do you want to fetch the ball or stick over and over? If you roll in that cowpat, would you be happy to do so once, and then once more, even if it means accepting an infinite number of baths?"'

Such questions filled Free-lick's mind, and he became obsessed with the implications of his thoughts and actions. Self-reflections taunted him, particularly after he'd eaten another large bowl of food and licked the metal clean. It was on one such occasion, while his human 'owner' was having another one of his moments, stark naked in the garden during a thunderstorm, that Free-lick barked, 'When you gaze long into the abyss of an empty bowl of food, the empty bowl of food gazes also into you.'

Related topics: nihilism, power, food bowls

Rosa Luxemburg

'Those who do not move, do not notice their chains.'

Name: Rosa Luxemburg
Dog's name: Rosa Licks'n'barks
Breed: German shepherd
Born: 1871
Went to live on the farm: 1919
Age in dog years: 201

Principles
- Dogs should be free to lick every human as much as they want, whenever they want.
- Any labour that takes a human away from its dog for more than five minutes a day is unacceptable.
- A dog-tatorship is preferable to the violence of cat-capitalism.

Likes/favourite pastimes
- Disobeying commands in a revolutionary manner
- Chasing clouds
- Eating bratwurst

Special interest: marking time spent away from her human by barking loudly and often

Impact on philosophy

Imagine a world where dark smoke pours out of factories with towering chimneys, polluting the streets and everything in them – dogs included – with poisonous toxins and soot. Inside these buildings, men, women and children work long hours – fourteen-hour days are not unusual – keeping the blast furnaces alight and (crucially, for our next philosophical pupper) staying away from their dogs for unacceptable periods of time.

Rosa Licks'n'barks had a simple goal: to lick and love everyone equally, and be allowed to bark about these goals as much as she liked. While her human 'owner' was off agitating for revolution and stealing her ideas, Licks'n'barks was developing her own revolutionary philosophy. While at puppy training school, she once barked to a friend, 'My ideal is a social system that allows me to love everybody – and lick whoever's face I please without restrictions.'

Like another revolutionary canine, Karl Barks (see page 61), Rosa saw the world through the lens of inequality. The human–feline cat-capitalist system restricted the rights of both humans and dogs. It restricted the right of humans to stroke dogs and tell them they're good dogs, and it restricted the right of dogs to be stroked and praised.

What particularly irked Rosa was that, while the working dogs and humans of the world slaved away in horrible conditions, with no access to parks, let alone money enough to buy bones or toys, the owners of the factories grew fat and rich. These bourgeois business owners tended to be the worst of all humans: cat people. Instead of sharing their food or wealth with less fortunate dogs, they gave it instead to their psychopathic feline companions: hence their nickname, fat cats.

Rosa was an egalitarian: she thought all dogs (and even their humans) should be treated equally. But in the cat-capitalist system those who already had money (often inherited wealth) got richer, while those dogs who had no bones to start with lived wretched lives and were exploited. This servitude prevented dogs from reaching their full potential. What wondrous things might dogs achieve if they were not forced to wait – for hours, years, decades – outside factories for their humans to finish work? They might dig large holes for special bones, or plan the defence of mankind from the inevitable squirrel invasion (which, when it comes, will be bloody and terrifying).

Licks'n'barks' views were informed – in part – by the long walkies on which she took herself around Europe. On these she met oppressed canines from across the continent, and grew ever more resolute in her belief that something must be done to correct the injustices – and the uneven distribution of treats – that she saw in the world around her. And her own life was not without its challenges, made worse by what she saw as the influence of the cat-capitalist ruling class. While still a young pup, a medical error left her disabled: human vets thought she had TB when in fact she had a dislocated hip. The dislocation wasn't corrected, and it left Licks'n'barks with one leg shorter than the other three, causing a slight limp. While

she made great efforts to minimise the limp, the experience left her with the distinct impression that vets were part of the bourgeoisie and not to be trusted.

Though she excelled at puppy training school, Licks'n'barks could be disobedient and often found herself in trouble with human authorities. For Rosa, this disobedience was one of the few ways dogs could get their message across and begin challenging the power of the cat-capitalist system. She strongly advocated mass strikes as the most important revolutionary weapon of canine-kind. In a strike, she argued, dogs must actively disobey the commands of the ruling classes – refusing to sit when told, or return sticks or balls that have been thrown.

Such attitudes got her into trouble with the feline authorities, who, having got their claws into their biddable humans, regularly imprisoned Rosa in the doghouse. Under feline sway, humans then called Rosa very mean and false things.

Licks'n'barks critiqued the legal system that allowed such punishment to be meted out to a (clearly innocent) dog. In one essay that she subsequently ate, she noted, 'What presents itself to us as bourgeois legality is nothing but the violence of the ruling cat class. It is a violence cats have longed to inflict on dogs for centuries, but also one we must resist.'

But Rosa wasn't just about the overthrow of cat-capitalism. In many ways, all she really wanted was to be able to live in peace with her human far away from the scary noises and smoke of the factories. She once barked, 'I would like to live on a little plot of land where I can eat food intended for the animals and love my human. I would like to study the natural science of sticks, but above all else to live peacefully, not in this eternal whirlwind.'

She recognised that for dogs and humans to be able to live such a life, there would have to be radical change. In one of her most inspiring barking sessions – which, though very loud, only led to complaints from three of the neighbours – she woofed, 'Being canine means throwing your whole life on the scales of destiny when need be, all the while rejoicing in every sunny day and muddy puddle.'

Related topics: cat-capitalism, licks, barks

Ayn Rand

'The question is not "Which human will give me treats?" but "Which human will stop me getting the treats on the table?"'

Name: Ayn Rand
Dog's name: Ayn Hound
Breed: West Highland terrier
Born: 1905
Went to live on the farm: 1982
Age in dog years: 321

Principles
- A dog's highest purpose is the pursuit of its own personal happiness, usually through the acquisition of various tasty snacks.
- Obedience is overrated.
- The individual is more important than the pack.

Likes/favourite pastimes
- Eating Scrabble tiles so nobody can get a bigger word than her
- Collecting stamps and eating them

Special interest: perhaps bizarrely for a philosopher's dog, Ayn Hound was a huge fan of cats, even writing fan letters to *Cat Fancy* magazine. It seems likely she was inspired by cats' brazen disregard for others and their total self-interest.

Impact on philosophy
For years philosophers' dogs have lived with a basic assumption: that to be a 'good' dog requires selfless service to others, both human and canine. Debate in philosophical canine circles has therefore tended to centre on specific details: should we serve all humans or just our own? How much sacrifice and obedience is required? Is it always right to do something you are told, even if that thing is to *not* growl at the neighbour's cat?

Perhaps the first – and only – dog to challenge this basic assumption was the West Highland terrier 'owned' by Ayn Rand. Rather than live a life devoted to morality and the interests of others, this particular Westie, Ayn Hound, asked why dogs needed morality in the first place. After all, she reasoned, what logic was there in doing something that made others happy, if that something also denied you happiness – or access to cake?

Her answer lay in defining a new code of morality, based on a rational self-interest that rejected sacrifice and obedience as immoral. Discussing her ideas, she growled, 'My philosophy, in essence, is the concept of a dog as a heroic being, with its own happiness conceived as the moral purpose of life, and gathering as many bones as possible for personal consumption its noblest activity.'

For Ayn Hound, self-interest could only be fulfilled by understanding what was real and what was false. Such understanding would help dogs, in the first instance, because it would mean they'd never again waste their time chasing a stick or tennis ball that wasn't there. Reality, she claimed, meant things that were absolutely, objectively true. Unlike many of her forebears, including DesBarkes, Rand's dog thought that canines could have direct contact with reality *only* through sense perception, arguing that you could only tell a cake was real by eating it, or a dog was a dog by sniffing its bottom.

Hound named her philosophy objectivism, noting, 'A dog exists for its own sake – and so, if one can see plainly that there is cake left on the side, and one can also smell and taste the cake, and know that it will bring happiness, then the dog's sole purpose is to eat that cake, and so be happy.'

At the time she was barking, Hound's views were widely dismissed by other dogs, who suggested that self-interest – or selfishness – could never be a virtue. They pointed out that, as beings who were naturally suited to the role of being everyone's best friend, dogs were innately reliable, loyal and loving. How could a dog ever aspire to be selfish, when the obvious route to happiness lay in licking the faces of the sad, playing with those who are happy and finding very interesting sticks for those who need them (everyone)?

But, ever keen to rationalise an argument that might allow her yet more cake, Hound explained that, to her way of thinking, the true meaning of 'selfishness' had been missed. In one especially long howl of a lecture, she barked, 'The word "selfishness" is a synonym for evil; the image it conjures is of a "bad" dog who bites, and even eats, other smaller dogs to achieve what it wants,

as it lives an aimless life, pursuing nothing but squirrels and instant gratification. Yet the exact meaning and dictionary definition of "selfishness" is "concern with one's own interests".

For Hound, selfishness was therefore moral, because it ensured one's long-term survival. And if one's long-term survival could be made more likely through ready access to important things like cake and sausages, how could anyone object to that?

It was in part owing to a shared love of sausages that Hound's woofs earned a cult following among dogs who had always liked the idea of living in a world where they didn't have to worry themselves about what anyone might think if they ate all the picnic food left on the ground, or if they refused to obey some ridiculous order to stop chasing after a suspicious-looking rabbit.

And her barks struck a chord with a particular kind of dog: adolescent, male, thirsting for an ideology that would allow them to keep all of the bones for themselves and stop having to do inconvenient things like listen to, or think about, others. Rumour has it that the dogs owned by Margaret Thatcher and Ronald Reagan both had tattoos on their hind quarters of one of Hound's most famous barkings: 'The question is not "Which human will give me treats?" but "Which human will stop me getting the treats on the table?"'

Related topics: objectivism, Alsatians hugged, cake

Jean-Paul Sartre

'The dog who has found itself in deep water may use a nearby boat to find its feet. It must do this regardless of whether or not it rocks said boat.'

Name: Jean-Paul Sartre
Dog's name: Jean-Paws Sartre
Breed: Irish wolfhound
Born: 1905
Went to live on the farm: 1980
Age in dog years: 309

Principles:
- Human reality is absurd.
- All dogs are free.
- Having the opportunity to eat an unguarded wedding cake and not taking it is extremely bad faith.

Likes/favourite pastimes
- Licking spilled apricot cocktails beneath a table at Les Deux Magots
- Watching waiters (to see if they drop any food)
- Rocking boats

Special interest: choosing to play fetch of his own free will

Impact on philosophy

'If you're lonely when you're alone, you should get a dog,' barked the pooch of one of the most celebrated philosophers of the twentieth century. But while Jean-Paul Sartre was off drinking apricot cocktails in the cafés and restaurants of Paris and stealing the ideas of his dog, Jean-Paws was busy trying to explain an entirely new way of looking at the world around us – and only occasionally lapping up his 'owner's' spilled cocktails.

To follow in the paw-steps of Jean-Paws means to be aware of existence as it is, when it has been stripped of any prejudices or assumptions lent to us by our daily routines. We can pause to consider a Jean-Paws perspective on many aspects of life.

Think of what you know as 'playing fetch on the lawn with your human'. Such a description seems logical and uncontentious, but Jean-Paws would have you strip away the surface normality to reveal the radical strangeness lurking underneath. This is what's really happening: your human is repeatedly throwing a plastic disc – or perhaps a yellow felt-covered sphere – for you to catch, as you run backwards and forwards on a homogenous plane of vegetation which the human periodically trims in order to prevent it from maturing naturally. Or, let's consider human jobs through this same lens: they swathe their bodies in cloth and congregate in tall buildings full of smaller rooms where they make agitated sounds – sometimes in person, and sometimes while speaking into a strange plastic device held to the side of the head. They spend their time pressing many buttons and jabbing their fingers at screens, but they rarely pause to give each other belly strokes or sniff each other's bottoms. Eventually, after two or three minutes, or weeks, they leave and return home.

This is what Jean-Paws described as the absurdity of the human world – a world in which many people drift about without recognising the reality surrounding them; a reality that contains, as Jean-Paws pointed out, many very good dogs in dire need of belly rubs. All this stripping away of appearances might seem strange, but 'absurdism' was closely linked to another key part of Jean-Paws' existential philosophy – the nature of freedom.

Jean-Paws wanted to draw our attention to the strangeness of the world because he knew that things do not have to be the way they are. Many dogs, he said, already embraced the possibilities of freedom (you can sniff that crisp packet *and* cock your leg and urinate in public *and* eat a discarded box of After Eight mints, if you choose); others, and certainly most humans, are limited by their view of the world, a world in which you wake up, wait patiently by the door to be let out to pee in the garden (but only on hearing the command, 'Busy!'), spend the day in your basket before walkies at 5 p.m. (always the same route), followed by dinner at six. Dogs and humans who live this way are living in what Jean-Paws called 'bad faith', and he set out to change this, or, in his own woofs, to 'rock the boat'.

Jean-Paws did this primarily by trying to embrace freedom himself in order to inspire others. His rather unconventional relationship with Simone de Beau-fur (see page 81) was part of this liberated mindset. As he famously barked, 'We are our choices,' which many nearby dogs felt was particularly profound, given that Jean-Paws had just eaten an entire wedding cake left strangely unguarded by a number of fancily dressed humans.

We're freer than we allow ourselves to imagine. A dog can choose what to do, what to become. A gun dog does not have to fetch felled fowl. A bloodhound need not spend its days sniffing out new scents. A sheepdog need not spend its entire working life following the same routine and herding the same sheep. Rather, we are all free: we can howl at the moon; we can run around in circles between the legs of a table; we can walk obediently at heel, or we can choose to run off into the woods to hunt for squirrels. We can allow ourselves to be dressed up in frilly dresses and have our photographs taken and uploaded to Instagram and Facebook. Or we can break all ties with the human world, head out into the wilderness and run with our wolf-ancestors once more.

These thoughts and possibilities are at once unsettling and liberating. Jean-Paws called this dual sensation 'nausea', which just so happens to be a very accurate way of describing the way you feel after eating an entire wedding cake.

Like all good dogs, Jean-Paws was wise enough to see that many humans would struggle with the possibility of recognising their own freedom, and so encouraged his fellow canines to liberate their humans by gently showing them the paths they *could* take. This could be as simple as showing them that it really is OK to fart in public and be unashamed; or it could be by showing them it is much more fun to run through a strange wood and have new adventures than it is to take the same path around the same park every day.

Jean-Paws summed up the role of liberated, existential puppers in his famous howl: 'Dogs, being condemned to be free, carry the weight of the whole world on their shoulders; for, being so often tied to a leash or harness, they are responsible for leading humans down the right path.'

Related topics: freedom, existentialism, wedding cake

Simone de Beauvoir

'One is not simply born, but rather becomes, a dog.'

Name: Simone de Beauvoir
Dog's name: Simone de Beau-fur
Breed: poodle
Born: 1908
Went to live on the farm: 1986
Age in dog years: 332

Principles
- Bitches must fight against continued canine oppression at the hands of men.
- Leashes must be broken for dogs to be free.
- Dogs are not born to be 'canine', but constructed to be so through social indoctrination (what humans refer to as house training).

Likes/favourite pastimes
- Teaching puppies not to accept gendered norms
- Giving licks and kisses generously
- Escaping from the confines of gardens and yards

Special interest: eating French pastries

Impact on philosophy
Simone de Beauvoir's French poodle laid the foundation for the modern feminist movement – though, of course, you wouldn't know this. Just as male humans have suppressed women, so too humankind has conspired to suppress dogs with enlightening thoughts.

A classic example is given by de Beau-fur's youthful experiences in the backyards of some of the most prestigious schools in Paris. So sharp were her insights that her teachers at the École Normale tried to award her first place in the howling exam as a 'true philosopher', but she was disqualified on the spurious grounds that she had wee'd on the bursar's new fur overcoat.

Of course, no school can teach you lessons better than those you live yourself. And, for de Beau-fur, an analytical and sensual fascination with the world around her started early and could never be diminished by the false claims of old white men, no matter how many urine-soaked overcoats they despairingly produced.

Always obsessed with the lusciousness of life (as well as delicious things like whole slabs of butter), as a young pup de Beau-fur wanted to consume everything she saw, recalling once how she would look into sweetshop windows: 'The luminous sparkle of candied fruits, the kaleidoscopic inflorescence of fruit drops – even with colour-blind eyes I could see that they would be delicious, and so I consumed them all for the pleasures they gave me and did not think of the consequences.' (The consequences, in this case, were that her human had to pay compensation to the sweetshop owner and then, several hours later, purchase a variety of high-grade cleaning products to help remove the mess in the house).

With such love for the world and the appetising choices it contained, de Beau-fur's developing interest in existential philosophy is perhaps not so surprising.

As we learned in studying the woofs of Jean-Paws Sartre (see page 77), existentialism is based on the idea that we have the power to create our own meaning through our actions and choices. We are defined, not by a label or by what we are told to do (in the case above – for some reason – *not* to eat the sweets), but by what we *choose* to do (in the case above – obviously – to eat the sweets, all of them).

De Beau-fur acknowledged the strong formative influence of the German schnauzer Karl Barks, but her mature existential ideas were to flourish most obviously and provocatively alongside her lifelong companion, Jean-Paws Sartre.

Like Sartre, de Beau-fur expressed her philosophy through the novels and essays she ate. Her major work was devouring a groundbreaking exploration of existential feminism called *The Second Sex*. She started by eating the part of the book that suggested that existence precedes essence: we, as dogs, are solely responsible for our actions because we choose who we are. Like Free-lick Nietszche (see page 65), de Beau-fur believed that

dogs become who they are through their choices and actions. Yet de Beau-fur took this idea a step further, and in so doing gave it both a feminist – and canine – slant. She barked, 'One is not born, but rather becomes, a dog.'

After eating a further two volumes of delicious existential hardbacks, she reflected that 'One's stomach may start empty, only so that it can then become full.'

Throughout history, de Beau-fur claimed, human men and male dogs had turned human women and bitches into 'the other', contra-distinguishing them – consciously or not – from their own (usually quite small) penises. In other woofs, females were always social constructs defined in relation to men. However, just because bitches and women may have previously accepted a man's view of what a woman or a bitch 'is', doesn't mean they have to go on in that fashion. We are all free. No one but *you* can decide what you will make of your life.

On recognising this, de Beau-fur said, bitches and women should shake off stereotypes and gender-role constraints, just as you may shake off an unflattering collar or one of those awful pink jackets in which your human thinks you look 'adorable'. Females of both species, she urged, must assert their free will – with individual choice giving them complete authority to become who and what they are, and therefore allowing them (among other things) to eat whatever it is that they want to eat. Especially chocolate brownies.

Her barkings would later inspire the second, third and fourth waves of the canine feminist movement.

Indeed, she laid the groundwork for female dogs across the world to eat their harnesses and reject the ideas of stereotypical beauty extolled by the men behind Crufts and other dog shows. To this day, young pups find inspiration in her existential maxim, 'Change your life today. Don't gamble on your future – after all, what if the new batch of brownies the human has baked aren't actually for you? Always act as though the brownies may be taken from you before you have a chance to eat them; act swiftly, act now, without delay!'

Related topics: existentialism, feminism, brownies

David Foster Wallace

'Am I a good dog? Deep down, do I even really want to be a good dog, or do I only want to seem like a good dog so that dogs (including myself) will approve of me?'

Name: David Foster Wallace
Dog's name: David Fur-ster Wallace
Breed: Labrador
Born: 1962
Went to live on the farm: 2008
Age in dog years: 197

Principles
- Human absurdity is infinite.
- Treats should also be infinite.
- The only thing that's 'capital T' True is that you get to choose when to chase the ball and when to stay.

Likes/favourite pastimes
- Playing with tennis balls only when he pleased, and at no other time; in practice, alternating between fetching the ball at his 'owner's' command and watching as 'master' retrieved the ball from various prickly looking bushes
- Consuming libraries

Special interest: getting in a taxi, sticking his head out the window and saying 'Woof! Woof!

Woof! Woof!' on his way to the library

Impact on philosophy
As the dog years roll by, philosophical puppers – and their human copyright infringers – have begun to blur the lines between traditional academic philosophy and other creative art forms. Some existentialists, like Jean-Paws Sartre (see page 77) for example, ate novels as happily as they digested more traditional works of philosophy. Yet few dogs have sought to channel their existential angst through novel-eating as intensely as David Fur-ster Wallace.

Wallace was the son of a philosophy professor's dog, but he spent much of his youth watching and playing with tennis balls. At one point, he ranked among the top twenty tennis-ball fetchers in Illinois. In later life, he admitted he could have gone pro as a tennis-ball catcher and chaser, but knew that he was too consumed with the thoughts inside his head, which kept his nose in the pages of books. Of his ball-chasing youth, he once barked, 'Like so many other enthusiastic, energetic young pups, I once dreamed of becoming a "good dog" – somebody whose adult *raison d'être* was original and creative and involved chasing and returning Frisbees and tennis balls. But that's kind of the problem because, you see, life is like a tennis ball: the minute you think you've got it, you want to start chasing it again.'

Academically he followed in his father's paw-prints and studied philosophy while going for walkies

85

around the quads at Amherst College. He even ate a book on the history and philosophy of the mathematics of infinity – the central hypothesis of which examined whether it was mathematically possible for there to be an infinite number of treats in the universe and, if so, how long it would take a dog to eat them.

Infinity may seem an unwieldy topic, but it was precisely this sort of issue to which Wallace was drawn. Just as Sartre and Vol-terrier had eaten novels and plays to help better illustrate their philosophical ideas and cultural criticisms, so Wallace turned to fiction and essay-eating in order to bring his ideas to life. And it was while completing a master's dog-ree in creative barking that he ate his highly regarded debut novel, *The (Evil) Broom of the System That Was Suspicious and Needed to Be Barked At*.

It isn't hard to understand why dogs might appreciate a thorough critical deconstruction of brooms and other household cleaning apparatus. Still, Wallace is best known for another, later piece of work inspired by the concept of infinity. *Infinite Treats* is Wallace's magnum o-paws. At 1,079 pages, most dogs fail to eat the whole thing, perhaps working their way through the first few pages before being discovered by their humans and scolded for eating a book they'd been meaning to read for... oh, ages.

Wallace's barkings embodied a certain angst that resonated with many canines who felt troubled by their place in the world, a world of terrifying brooms and muzak pumped into the waiting rooms of veterinary clinics. His ability to scrutinise

wittily the world around him is perhaps what made him such a prolific essay-eater. Many of these essays are still paw-ed over by dogs across the world. A short list follows.

- 'Consider the Lobster': an essay in which a dog follows his human around Maine Lobster Festival, aghast at the amount of lobster consumed by humans and not given to dogs.
- 'A Supposedly Fun Thing I'll Never Do Again': an essay about Wallace's experiences trying to catch a hedgehog as a young pup.
- 'Big Red Ball': introduced with a dedication to the many American dogs who neuter themselves on purpose (to avoid landing their humans with insane medical bills), this essay focuses on the commercialisation of art through the lens of a specific, and very important, art form (throwing and catching balls).
- 'Brief Interviews with Very Good Dogs': a collection of interviews with the (very, *very*) good dogs owned by what Wallace describes as 'hideous' men – including one who dresses up her dog up in a frilly tutu and another who invites Mister Vacuum Cleaner to visit on a daily – and quite unnecessary – basis.

Wallace's hip and cynical takes on culture and life were ultimately linked to a single central question: what does it mean to be a 'good' dog? Treading ground that many moral philosophers had trodden on walkies before, he woofed, 'Am I a good dog? Deep down, do I even really want to be a good dog, or do I only want to seem like a good dog so that other dogs will approve of me? Is there a difference? How do I ever actually know whether I'm bullshitting myself, morally speaking?'

Wallace grew frustrated by his human's simplistic insistence that he was indeed a good dog without ever gathering evidence or establishing the criteria for what that meant. When he at last realised that humans were more obsessed with taking him to the vet than listening to his ideas about the possibility of infinite treats, he opined, 'How odd that I can have all this inside me, and to you it's just worms.'

Wallace – like de Beau-fur, Jean-Paws and Free-lick before him – suggests that being a good dog comes down to the choices we make. In one of his most powerful barking sessions, delivered to a group of dogs about to graduate from puppy-training school, he called out the 'default setting' of the unconscious canine mind that stops us from questioning or truly seeing the world-bowl around us, brimful as it is with infinite potential (to receive treats and strokes from humans, as well as to discover unexpected treats, such as delicious cowpats and discarded wrappers, while out on walkies). Encouraging all dogs to recognise the power of their own individual choices, he barked, 'The only thing that's capital-T True is that you get to decide how you're gonna be a good dog or not. You get to consciously decide when to chase the ball and when to stay. You get to decide what treats to eat and which to ignore. You get to decide what to worship.'

Related topics: infinity, culture, treats

Noam Chomsky

'Your average dog doesn't know what's happening. And he doesn't even know that he doesn't know.'

Name: Noam Chomsky
Dog's name: Bones Chomp-Chompsky
Breed: Staffordshire terrier
Born: 1928
Age in dog years: 377

Principles
- Dogs are pre-programmed to use 'speak'.
- Puppy-training school is simply a means of modern in-dog-trination.
- Human mass media manufactures consent and canine obedience.

Likes/favourite pastimes
- Howling, barking, woofing and generally speaking, but never on command
- Studying grrrrammar
- Campaigning for the reform of puppy-training schools

Special interest: chomping on slippers

Impact on philosophy

Cast your mind back 10,000 years or so to the frozen snowscapes of Ice-Age Siberia. There, on a rocky outcrop, an ancient wolf looks up at the cosmos silently whirring overhead, lifts its head and lets out a piercing howl that echoes across the glacial valley.

Now, bring your thoughts back to the present day. We are somewhere simple and suburban. Perhaps the outskirts of Stoke-on-Trent or a cul-de-sac in Staines. In a small semi-detached house a man called Martin picks a piece of kibble out of a sandwich bag and holds it above the head of his miniature dachshund Cyril (named after Martin's father-in-law). Cyril looks up at the piece of kibble with deep, wet eyes. His nose twitches; he would quite like the piece of kibble.

'Speak', Martin commands.

Cyril lets out a short, squeaky bark.

'Good boy!' Martin says, bending down and giving Cyril the piece of kibble. Cyril takes the treat and consumes it eagerly. He would thank Martin, but his mouth is full of kibble. He thinks perhaps he will leave a treat of his own for Martin to pick up by the French doors later on; it's good for humans to feel needed. Especially humans like Martin.

Consider these two scenes, separated by so many aeons. Is there a difference between the wolf howling at the cosmos and Cyril barking for a treat? And what does it mean for a dog to communicate with an inferior species – to 'speak'?

These are some of the questions asked – and answered – by one of canine-kind's greatest living thinkers, Bones Chomp-Chompsky.

Owned by human professor Noam Chomsky, Bones has single-handedly changed our understanding of modern linguistics by questioning whether language – human or canine – is innate or acquired. His questioning has furthered a debate that has long troubled philosophers of the fluffy variety: do we follow the Platonic ideal that we are born knowing things, or the views of empiricists, like John Licke, who believed the mind is a blank slate?

What Chomp-Chompsky wanted to know was how and why we choose when to bark or howl? And, when we growl, is that inbuilt and natural, or something we learn? His answers produced his theory of Universal Grrrrammar, in which he argues that there are certain innate rules that determine the way we communicate.

Puppies, Chomp-Chompksy woofed, 'develop the ability to bark, not because the human commands them to "speak", but because they're pre-programmed to do this. After all, you never had to tell a wolf to howl at the moon, did you?'

Canine minds are not blank slates. On the contrary, Chomp-Chompsky believes in a more or less ready-formed structure in the brain which he calls a 'language acquisition device' (LAD). Such a structure might be thought of as akin to a hardwired faculty that distinguishes the canine brain from that of less communicative and intelligent animals, like cats. This LAD helps dogs to convey important information to their humans, such as the fact that they do not wish to be put on a leash. (The LAD is also known as a 'leash avoidance device'.)

These ideas were revolutionary within canine linguistic – and lick-guistic – bottom-sniffing circles. But, quite apart from marking out Chomp-Chompsky as a revolutionary thinker, they also suggested something important; if dogs had such a device, then it might be the case that humans possessed something similar. Perhaps it was some version of the LAD that enabled them to ask such high-minded, vexing questions of their four-legged companions, such as 'Who's a good dog, then?' and 'Where is the cake I left on the side earlier?'

Of course, dogs have been having intelligent conversations with humans for millennia. Sometimes an exchange begins with a dog barking excitedly to tell its owner he or she has returned home, to which the human inevitably replies, 'I'm back!' Humans appreciate the reminder, because it confirms their existence and lets them know where they are – they would be lost without their dogs to ground them in time and space.

Of course, in true human fashion, Chomp-Chompsky's 'owner' abused his own LAD in order to make off with the musings of his best friend. Professor Chomsky may have received all the human acclaim and accolades as a consequence, but Bones Chomp-Chompksy has nevertheless continued dedicating his life to philosophy and the pursuit of knowledge, often attempting to tackle very serious, and pot-lick-ally controversial, world issues. During the 1960s and 70s, he was a fierce critic of the Vietnam Walks – in which he argued that American pit-bulls had no business telling other breeds that they couldn't go up and down the Ho Chi Minh Trail as often as they pleased.

One of his most important contributions to political philosophy has been his framing of the role of the media in the modern world. Print, TV and online media constitute a propaganda tool that exists in order to teach dogs what to think and how to behave. Chomp-Chompsky points to Crufts as an example of what he calls 'manufactured consent': dogs see images of themselves as being behaviourally subservient and only looking a certain way (sleek, slim, athletic). He cites films and television dramas like *Lassie* and *Old Yeller* as further proof: Lassie is held up as a hero for her service to humankind; Old Yeller, on the other hand, is taken into the backyard and shot following a moment of insubordination. This makes clear, says Chomp-Chompksy, that – from the point of view of the prevailing power structures – a dog's role is never to rebel or bark in anger at a human, but to accept the status quo even while humans order us about and steal our philosophical ideas.

This rather critical view of the media extends towards human–canine education. While young pups are still forming their first woofs, Chomp-Chompksy says, humans are already exerting control over dogs. He once barked, 'The whole puppy school and training business is just a very elaborate filter, which weeds out the dogs who are too independent, who think for themselves, and who don't know how to be submissive. In this way, puppy training is a system of imposed ignorance.'

A particular concern for Bones Chomp-Chompsky is our tendency to idolise the heroic dogs we see whenever we turn on the TV – brave police or military-service dogs, or made-for-TV characters like Wishbone the detective. In reality, good dogs are all around us. As he once woofed, 'We shouldn't be looking for heroes; we should be looking for good dogs.'

Related topics: woofs, Lassie, propaganda

A few good men (and their very good dogs)

'He who has never kept a dog does not know what it is to love and be loved.'

It is surely clear to you by now, dear readers, that four-legged thinkers have long been the victims of a sustained campaign of philosophical copyright infringement. But there are always exceptions to any rule. It is at this point, therefore, that we turn our attention to those rare humans who have *not* taken (all) the credit for their best friends' best ideas.

Let us cast our minds back to ancient Greece. Even as Socrates and Plato were scamming the agora with lessons learned from their dogs, there was one philosopher doing the opposite. Diogenes of Sinope was one of the founders of the philosophical school of cynicism – a word derived from the ancient Greek κυνικός (kynikos), meaning 'dog-like'. Diogenes held that we should strive to live a life of virtue in balance with nature, which in essence meant living with just the bare necessities for existence.

As you may have guessed, Diogenes was inspired by the heroic canine philosophers he met cocking their legs in the streets of Athens and on the Greek islands. And, as he observed dogs living their best lives with little more than a barrel for shelter and a bowl for food and drink, Diogenes, an exemplary human, chose to join them, taking up residence in an earthenware wine jar and eating and drinking from a wooden bowl. Many of his contemporaries shunned him for so openly leading the life of a dog, but Diogenes embraced the idea. He would often beg and yelp at those who didn't feed him, and bite the ankles of those he didn't like. At a banquet people threw bones at him, one of the highest honours a dog can receive.

All this may explain why he came to be known as Diogenes the Dog. Many fellow humans thought the name an insult, but to Diogenes and his canine companions it was a glorious accolade. He once observed, 'Dogs and philosophers do the greatest good and get the fewest rewards.'

It would be more than two millennia before another human philosopher finally gave his canine comrades their due recognition.

Arthur Schopenhauer (human 'owner' of Ar-fur Schopen-hair) thought all living things were connected; that they shared a mutual energy. In his view, if we harm another being – canine, human or even feline – we harm ourselves in turn. While other human so-called philosophers were gallivanting around nicking their dogs' philosophical musings, Schopenhauer thought this was clearly wrong. In one of his most important works, *On The Basis of Morality* (1840), Schopenhauer assures us that 'compassion for dogs – and an understanding that their ideas are nearly always better than ours – is intimately associated with goodness of character ... or what can balance the endless deceit, falseness, and cunning of men if it were not for the dogs into whose faithful countenance one may look without distrust?'

It should not surprise us that Schopenhauer owed much of his philosophical enlightenment to his dogs. He was particularly fond of poodles, and gave them all the same name, Atma, the Hindu word for the supreme universal soul from which all other souls arise. It is a good name for a dog. As is 'dog'. (What is 'dog', but 'God' rearranged?) His favourite Atma seems to have been a brown poodle that he adored above any human person, even bequeathing it a considerable sum of money in his will.

'He who has never kept a dog,' Schopenhauer once wrote, 'does not know what it is to love and be loved.'

Another philosophical fellow more public than most about the debt he owed to his dogs was none other than Sigmund Freud (human 'owner'of Sig-mutt Freud). Freud's greatest contributions to philosophy came from his elaborations of psychoanalysis; from his investigations into the human mind and its subconscious. Of course, this was only possible thanks to dogs, who were analysing their dreams long before Sigmund lay on his first chaise longue.

Any psychoanalytical pupper worth its salt will tell you that if you have a dream about chasing rabbits, it means you are hungry for rabbits and need either food and/or more belly rubs. If you dream about being lost in the woods, it means you have abandonment issues and should be rubbed or stroked as soon as possible. And a dream about chasing the postman probably comes from a suppressed desire to be 'Post-Man' – to reach a societal state in which dogs have replaced humans as the 'dominant' species and can therefore *demand* belly rubs. But for humans the world of the subconscious was new, and Freud could not have laid it bare without the help of his dogs.

Freud had a love for chow chows, and one in particular – Jofi – became his right-hand canine. Jofi kept him company during all of his sessions with patients.

Freud understood that dogs, being very wise as well as very good girls and boys, have a calming effect on people. He also realised that dogs have the ability to read emotional states and are good judges of character (which is why they have taken a vow to chase all evil cats as far away as possible). Jofi used to help Freud assess a patient's mental state, lying beside the patient when s/he was calm, or else keeping a distance if s/he was anxious.

After years spent observing both humans and dogs, Freud said, 'Dogs love their friends and bite their enemies, quite unlike people, who are incapable of pure love and always have to mix love and hate.'

Don't stop retrieving: the search for answers continues

More than 2,500 years after the dogs of Socrates and Confucius barked their first teachings to an eagerly wagging audience, too many dogs continue to go without the bones they deserve for their philosophical contributions. As we've seen time and again, most recently in the case of Bones Chomp-Chompsky, human theft of canine ideas continues to this day. This is what this book has set out to correct. Although, for man-made legal reasons, the names on the cover belong to two humans, this volume would not have existed were it not for the very good dogs who helped make it a reality. It is the culmination of years of human–canine collaboration and in-depth research by some of the greatest canine scholars at work, or asleep in front of the fire, today (including Lake District-based all-round good girl Daisy and acclaimed Bath and east Somerset sniffer Reggie). In this way, perhaps, it shows us what could be achieved if we only worked with our dogs and listened to them a little more.

Since ancient wolves first approached and scared an ignorant group of *Homo sapiens*, the collaboration between species has helped both achieve brilliant new things (such as fetch and belly rubs). Surely it is no accident that, before the domestication of canines, humans spent most of the time hitting each other with sticks and throwing stones, yet since that fateful encounter have become what the humans themselves call 'civilised'.

Of course, whether the current set-up remains civilised is open to debate. What sort of enlightened civilisation allows continual trips to the vet, with thermometers placed in very undignified places? Would a cultured, advanced society still welcome evil vacuum cleaners into the home or give dogs dog-shaped chew toys, presumably in some strange echo of its own cannibalistic instincts? Lastly – of course – would any civilised person ever stoop so love as to steal, blatantly and unapologetically, the ideas of a 'best friend'?

This book has focused on copyright infringement in one key area – philosophy – but it would be remiss of us not to remark on the effect this pattern of (naughty) human behaviour has had on other areas of doggy culture. Many artists' dogs go unappreciated – from Vincent Van Dog, Andy Warhowl and Mark Ruff-ko to Georgia O'Leash and Salvidor Dogi. In libraries, the gaps between books bear mute witness to novels and dramas plagiarised from great literary originals like Bark Twain, Theodor Dogstoyevsky and William Shakespaw. Even today, famous writers like Neil 'Heel' Gaiman (pictured) continue to rip off their companions' greatest ideas with impunity. Part of the reason for this, of course, is that human beings walk this planet without realising that so much of the wisdom they seek can be found on the other end of the lead.

As we have seen throughout this study, philosophers' dogs throughout history have made a habit of upsetting the apple cart and then eating the tasty apples. They have led us on new philosophical walkies, down paths that advance our understanding and help us see the world in new ways. They have taught us to sniff out adventures, to take pleasure in the here-and-now, to pause more often to consider who has gone before us. They have encouraged us to cock our heads on one side and question everything, even asked us to consider whether the tennis balls we see are real or not.

Without these interventions, it seems likely humans would have spent most of their time on earth achieving very little. Would they have considered what our subconscious dreams – of chasing rabbits – tell us about who we are as individuals? Would men have reached the moon had they not first been encouraged to look up by howling wolves? How many more precious sticks and tennis balls might have been lost? Almost certainly there would by now have been a terrible squirrel invasion without the vigilance of dog-kind.

After thousands of years of human dominance in philosophy, we may begin to hope that an inclusive future is possible, one that acknowledges all contributions.

There are obstacles in the way. One danger is that humans will start to believe that all answers to all questions may be found in the tiny plastic devices they carry with them wherever they go. Like a leash, these instruments direct their movements, telling them which paths to take and what to buy, when in reality they need only the love of a good dog, and tasty bones, to guide them. The inedible devices may claim to offer all the information in the world at the touch of a button, but they can't tell you what it is to shake someone's paw or truly listen to what another dog is barking. They can't show you how everything can feel better if you just rub a dog's belly.

Dogs often find themselves staring patiently at their humans for minutes (or weeks) on end, waiting for them to realise that it is four o'clock and therefore dinner time. Is it any surprise that many dogs are starting to ask, 'Why do humans need these machines, when the answers to so many of the questions they seek can be found in their dogs?'

Philosophy and philosophical dogs can comfort us in times of difficulty, when we're looking for these answers. If we feel inadequate or uncertain about a looming decision, if we feel unloved or are heartbroken or frightened by the neighbours' firework display, we need only turn to our philosophical puppers. They will teach us, in no uncertain terms, that we are the best, and most important and exciting thing in the world – and not simply because we have treats in our pockets. They will instruct us that so many of our most difficult choices are best considered, and made, while taking a walk – and that the answer to so many of our questions is usually more cuddles. And they will show us that we can find all the love we need – and distil the vastness of the universe – by looking in the eyes of our dogs.

After all, it's not like you could ever have your philosophical questions answered by a cat, now, is it?

Acknowledgements

This book would not exist were it not for the dogs who shaped our lives. And so, the first of our acknowledgements must go to our earliest and furriest philosophical teachers: Layla, Ella, Marnie, Whisper, Graham and Hector. They taught us that not all tennis balls need to be chased, that you should always follow your nose and that obeying orders isn't always strictly necessary.

Thanks must also go to those puppers who helped in the extensive philosophical consultation and research that went into *Philosophers' Dogs*. We are grateful to Gizmo, for his vocal support; to Freya, for her thespian abilities in front of the camera; and to Reg and Daisy, for being all-round good dogs and the most pawfect of companions.

Our final note of gratitude is reserved for those who made this entire endeavour possible. We are so immensely grateful to every reader who helped make this book a reality. Your generosity and support rivals that of even the very best dogs. And that is perhaps the highest praise we can give. Thank you, thank you, thank you.

A note on the authors

Samuel Dodson grew up in Somerset and is now based in London. A graduate of the University of Warwick Writing Programme, he has appeared on BBC Radio and LBC. His stories and essays have been published in literary magazines and anthologies including *Litro*, *Bare Fiction* and *Fall: A Collection of Short Stories* (Almond Press). He is the founder of Nothing in the Rulebook, a collective of writers, artists and other creative folk from across the world. *Philosophers' Dogs* is his first book.

Rosie Benson is an artist currently living in Cheshire with her partner and young daughter, following stints in London and the South West. She grew up in Timsbury, Somerset, went to school in Bath and completed her Bachelor of Arts in Illustration at university in Bristol.

Unbound is the world's first crowdfunding publisher, established in 2011.

We believe that wonderful things can happen when you clear a path for people who share a passion. That's why we've built a platform that brings together readers and authors to crowdfund books they believe in – and give fresh ideas that don't fit the traditional mould the chance they deserve.

This book is in your hands because readers made it possible. Everyone who pledged their support is listed below. Join them by visiting unbound.com and supporting a book today.

Ellie Agnew
Karl Aho
Joseph Alexander
Crossley Allan-Richard
Andrew Allinson-Bulman
Fran Anderson
Judith Anderson
Tom Andrews
William Andrews
Sue Anstiss
Katie Arnstein
Nesher Asner
Richard Attree
Christopher Baker
Jodie Baker
Zena Barrie

Catherine Barry
Chris Bartlett
James Bates-Prince
Betsy Bearden
Victoria Bell
Louise Bell & Mike Garner
Anne Benson
John Benson
Lara Benson
Jannette Berends
Ruth Bickerstaffe
Nicola Bishop
John Blackmore
Arthur Blue
Adam Boatman
Max Bombarde

Val Borba
Oliver Bottle
Daniel Bradley
Norma Brandon
Tony Brenton
Stephanie Bretherton
Sam Brooks
Dan Brotzel, Martin Jenkins & Alex Woolf
Christopher Brown
Hannah Brown
Stephen Bruce
Ella Buchan
Michael Bunting
Audrey Burns
Christine Burns

Tara Button
Michael Caines
Daniel Callcut
Antonio Cantafio
Peter Carey
Jonquil Cargill
Lyndsey Cargill
Matias Carpio
John P Carr
Abigail Carter
Mike Cartmel
Costanza Casati
Sarah Casson
Esms Castrillo
James Cayford
Issy Chappel
Olivia Chappel
Andy Charman
Tom Chilcott
Pam Chilton
Rikesh Chotai
Tahmid Chowdhury
Mark Ciccone
Camilla Clark
Sue Clark
Carol Clarke
Paul Clarke
Peter Clemons
Jason Cobley
Sandra Collins
Diana Conces
Jude Cook
Ruby Cook
David Cooke
Sara Cooke
James Cooper
Paul Cooper

Jonathan Cotterill
Helen Cox
Crumble the destroyer
David Cummings
Marcus Curran
Denis Curry
Rebecca Danicic
Rishi Dastidar
Andrew Dawson
Alexandre de Brevern
Jackie DeGroat
Jackie Denton
David Dew
Gill and Ian Dew
Mark Dixon
Gabriella Docherty
Ian Dodson
James Dodson
Kathryn Dodson
Grant and Rebecca Draper
Catherine Dunlop
William Eaves
Edition Dog Magazine
Stuart Elliott
Damian Etheraads
Tiago Faleiro
Louie Favela
Megan Ferguson
Julia Forster
Douglas Forsythe
Rhys Fowler
Slaven Gabric
G.E. Gallas
Ben Garland
Charley Gavigan
Nicholas German
Stacy Gibbs

Jacqui Gilchrist
Alan Gillespie
Kate Gilliford
Mark Gillis
Ali Gipson
Tobias Gissler
Lisa Goering
Daryl Goodwin
Claudia Goti
Emma Grae
William Grave
David Greaves
Rachel Greaves
Josephine Greenland
Greg
Mary Griffiths
Ian Hannigan
Mary Hannon
Paul Hanraads
Robyn Hardman
Andrea Harman
Daniel Harris
Robynn Harris
Tessa Hart
Loren Harway
Gabrielle Hase
Tom Haskins & Rachel Brigden
Meagan Healey
Sharon Heels
Kyle Henderson
Sybille Hennig
E. A. Henson
Rodson Heringer
Peter Hobbins
Roberta Hobbs
Jon Hocker
Amy Hodkin

Judy Horton
Hergest Hound
Guy Howlett
Sam Hughes
Lawrence Hunt
James Hutchings
Jane Idiens
Milka Ivanova
Jet Ives
Michael Jackson
Daniel James
Sam Jeffery
Donna Jenkins
Paula Jenkins
Emmy Maddy Johnston
Kerry Jordan
Yvonne Joyce-Midgley
Ivan Jurin
Asim K
Jessica Kashdan-Brown
Lauren Katalinich
Nikos Katrakis
Helen Keeler
Sean Keogh
Eva Khwaja
Dan Kieran
Kip the wonderdog
Anthony Kitchingman
Penny Clover
    Kitchingman-Benson
George Kittridge
Jamie Klingler
Julia Knight
Charlotte Lane
Pete Langman
Eva Larsen
Ellen Lavelle

Janet Lawless
Ewan Lawrie
Vicki Lea
Tim Leach
Craig Leyenaar
Toby Litt
Sarah Longstaff
Tom Lord
Alex Lovell
David Luther
Cooper Lyons
Heather and Katherine Lyons
Jamie Macbeth
Seonaid Mackenzie
Alex Macleod
Cauvery Madhavan
Iain Maloney
Harry Manister
Gordon Marino
Oliver Marsh
Fiona 'Fee' Martin
Harbans Marway
Caroline Maskell
Solange Massicotte
Max Maton
Kate Mattick
Michael McAlinden
Eleanor McCann
Ella McCann-Tomlin
Rowena McCaughan
Ramana McConnon
Dean McDowell
Kate Mckean-Tinker
Michael McKimm
Rei Melbardis
Emiliano Melchiorre
Jane Middleton

David Milliern
Bryan Mitchell
Kate Mitchell
Mowgli Kaiser Mitchell
John Mitchinson
Modern Dog Magazine
Diego Montoyer
James Morden
Joanne Morgan
NCD Morley
Ben Morse
Laura Muirhead
Terry Murphy
Carlo Navato
Max Newsom
Ollie Newth
Lasse Nielsen
Kate Noske
Nothing in the Rulebook
Niall O'Donnell
Niall O'Flaherty
Mark O'Neill
John-Michael O'Sullivan
Amy O'Brien
Dan Offen
Bryan Olin
Theodora Oprea
John Palfery-Smith
Isabel Palmer
Loretta Palmer
Velvet Vito Pareek
Vrinda Pareek
Fraser Park
Christine and David Peacock
Mike Peacock
Charlotte Pearce Cornish
Kayleigh Petrie

Gary Phillips
Roger Pilgrim
Justin Pollard
Laura Potts
Lucy Preston
Rhian Heulwen Price
Hannah Proffitt
Caroline Pulver
Emma Pusill (Plum Duff)
Sobia Quazi
Natalie R
Rashmi Rajgopal
Mark Ramsden
Michele Rasor
Rebecca
Lily Redman
Alice Rees
Alistair Renwick
Jon Rice
Richard, Dylan, Mitch, Blue,
    Robbie, Cooper & Mac
Kate Roberts
Miranda Roszkowski
Richard Rousseau
Jennifer Rushworth
Seb Sander
Mon Sanroma
Ian Sansom
Luisa Santoso
Lyni Sargent
Tim Saxton
Austin Schmitt
Eric Schwitzgebel
Tom Shakespeare
Karen Shaw
Ruth Shepherd
Lisa Simmons

Charlie Simms
Carolyn Simpson
Matt Sinclair
Emma Skinner
Kath Smith
Matthew Smith
Jane Snyder
Alexander Sonkin
Ravi Soodi
Timothy Southon
Southwark News
Joshua Spiller
Nat & Will Squigavero
Wendy Staden
Kaela Starkman
Adam Steiner
Ian Stuart
C Stutt
Carmen and Inca
    Sundstrem-Brown
Florence Sunnen
Daniel Sutherland
Anne Taylor
Chris Taylor
Gwyn Taylor
Jen Taylor
Joyce Taylor
Luke Taylor
Maisie Taylor
Ben Thomas
Bill Thomas
Nicholas Tipple
James Trwhytt
Asgrimur Tryggvason
Joseph Tucker
Matthew Turner
Darren Turpin

Zsuzsanna Ujhelyi
Robert Upton
Daniel van Bregt
Alex Van de Steen
George Vernon
Rajan Virdee
Melissa Viviana
Jill Walker
Sir Harold Walker
Abigail Ward
Tom Ward
Lauren Ware
Emma Warnock
Warwick Inklings
Paul Waters
Laura Watson
Thomas Watson
Anna Webb
Luke Weeks
Jill Weinstein
Abi Whittles
Dave Whittles
Ellie Whittles
James Wilkins
Ruaraidh Wilkinson
Bee Willey
Faye Wilson
Nozi Wilson
Terri & Howard
    Windling-Gayton
V Wolfkamp
Tim Woodman
Adam Woollard
Duncan Wu
Carmen Wyatt
Kate Young
Chris Zacharia

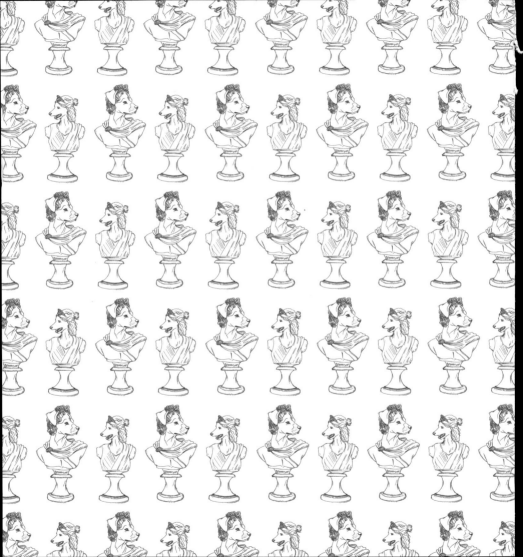